A

Woman's

WORTH

By Tonya Brown

Printed In the United States of America.

Book Editing by: Tonya Brown, Daron Brown, Asriel Brown, and Veronica Lee
Book Formatting by: Veronica Lee
Cover Design by: Angelina Blanks Brown,

My Dedication

This book is dedicated to ALL of the ladies in the world. May this testimony help you see the divinely ordained purpose that God has for your life. May you see yourself through the eyes of your Heavenly Father who created you and always esteem your worth in His sight.

I pray that this book will encourage you to never give up on your dreams of having your very own "Knight in Shining Armor."

He'll **WAIT**, honor, respect, and adore you!

If nobody has ever told you before, I want you to know that YOU'RE WORTH IT!

My Acknowledgements

I would first like to thank God the Father for choosing me to exemplify his goodness in such a glorious way.

I would also like to thank my Lord and Savior Jesus Christ for strengthening and enabling me to take on this task.

To my mother Lester A. Patterson, who has gone on to be with the Lord. You were truly my shero. You instilled in me the principles of hard work and perseverance. You taught and showed me the true love of God and for that I am eternally grateful. You were the first person I wanted to call when my book was finished. My GREATEST supporter! I love you Mom.

I would like to give a great big thank you to my Pastor Dr. Steve Houpe and his wife Dr. Donna Houpe for the sacrifice of time and energy that it took to teach me, and many others, the uncompromising Word of God. They were truly a part of my destiny.

I would like to show the greatest appreciation to my absolute best friend and encourager, my husband Darren who insisted that this testimony was so phenomenal that I needed to share it with the world. Without him, there would be no story. Honey I love you with the deepest love!

To our children, BJay, Ebony, Daron and Asriel, who were the greatest blessing to me during this journey. Caring for you gave me purpose and such joy. My desire to give you the best in life caused me to seek God for his divine wisdom and knowledge. Thank you so much. You were truly my inspiration.

Table of Contents

Foreword

I remember the day my eyes first fell upon Tonya. She was exiting the church sanctuary holding her youngest baby girl closely to her body. My attention, as always, was drawn to the baby, but this first encounter afforded me the opportunity to become acquainted with one of the most dynamic women I know. A mother of four beautiful children, an entrepreneur and a woman of incredible strength, is Tonya Brown.

Later, I came to hear bits and pieces of her story about her husband who was away in prison for many years. Yet, Tonya faithfully raised her children in the Word of God, miraculously sent them to a Christian School and waited with expectations for the day of her husband's return. What was she made of? I'm sure many people whispered. How could she stand in the midst of such opposition? Where did she get the strength to keep running? Why didn't she quit? A Woman's Worth will take you on the journey to discovering the answers to all of these questions and more!

The fortitude to stand beside her husband and the will to not quit are mere images of her life. You will discover as you embrace the story of Tonya and Darren Brown that nothing is impossible with God. You will be refueled and refreshed with hope to run again! Take this incredible journey with Tonya Brown as she guides you through *A Woman's Worth* and discover your inner beauty, strength and power! This book is a message of hope and a lifeline to so many who desire a change, but will only discover that it's possible through the testimony of another.

Dr. Donna Houpe
Harvest Church
Kansas City, MO

Do you not know I am a woman? I find my circumstances both amazing and powerful. A famous excerpt from Marianne Wilson said it best. "Who am I to be brilliant, gorgeous, talented or fabulous? Actually, who are you not to be?" I deserve absolute respect and acknowledgement. I am the true *shero* of humanity. I am worth the wait, because I understand, "A Woman's Worth!"

A woman's worth is unique in every way. Like a diamond it shines with its many facets giving clarity to its presence. Just as diamonds are rare and unique, there are people in this world who I believe are just like diamonds, divinely placed here on this Earth as though God's plan was to allow Himself to flow, breathe, move and have His very being in them. Although He is just, God seems to favor abundantly these intricate vessels of purpose; it seems as though give meaning to life, for whoever comes into contact with them. Because every human life is precious to God, we know that these peculiar, some may think strange creatures are gifts that reflect God's love to mankind, walking and living among us! Let me tell you about one such individual and although I may be a little biased, this beautiful person is my wife whom I've shared

26 years of marriage with. This woman, who gave me such unconditional love and support, endured pain and isolation, she loved me beyond all of my faults, and cried behind closed doors as God gathered her tears in a bottle preserved to produce a river of joy. She fought battles nobody knew about. Suffering that she endured because she believed there was a reason that was worth the effort. While you're reading this you may be thinking what's so special about her suffering? She did it trusting God for 16 years during my incarceration. This is her story of how she kept herself pure trusting in God's all sufficient grace to save her husband from himself and to help him find his way back to God. Do you believe in miracles? If you don't, you will after reading this story.

This book was written with you in mind, perhaps to bring about a miracle in your own life. As a matter of truth, I know this book will change the way you see yourself bringing clarity to life. So, don't just read this book, make it your own. Reflect and consider the thoughts you just read without rushing to the next chapter, because this book will make you want to do that. With that, let every woman and reader around the world brace yourself, find your perfect comfy spot, open up the pages of the this book and be lavished with truth and wisdom that unveils A WOMAN'S WORTH!

Darren Brown

Introduction

We learn best to listen to our own voices if we are listening at the same time to other women whose stories, for all our differences, turn out, if we listen well, to be our stories also.

-Barbara Damberg-

Ladies, let me tell you how I stood by his side, supported him, and watched the shackles that were holding him bound, fall off of him. Keep reading and see how God sustained us and how we came out on top.

And for that lady who's waiting, what do you do? How do you accept him back into your life, into YOUR world? How do you still respect him as the Head of your home, as the Priest God called him to be? How do you deal with the emotional scars (yours and his)? How can you help him to be successful and respected in his own home first, and also in the community? (Proverbs 31:23) What do you need to know about prison and how it affects the mind of a man? How do you cope? How do you wait? Should you wait? THE ANSWERS ARE IN THIS BOOK!

Read one woman's story of victory, through years of spiritual warfare, as she patiently waited 16 years for the man she loved. See how God took tragedy and turned it into triumph!

I attained the knowledge that I'm going to share with you while my husband was addicted to cocaine and later incarcerated for 16 years. The information however, is transferable to any area of your life – if you're lost, you'll find Jesus, if you're sick, you'll find healing, and if you're poor, you'll find out how to turn your situation around. The bottom line is, getting to know Jesus and understanding who you are in Christ transcends situations and circumstances. Once you **know** Him, you can win everyday and in everyway!

Anyone who takes the time to read this book and apply the principles will never be the same, be it man or woman. To the woman reader, you will end this book refreshed, enlightened, empowered, and feeling good about yourself; knowing WHO you are and WHOSE you are. You will understand your royal place in this kingdom and will not be afraid to demand your

"Queenship." You will never again bow to the 'less than' mentality because you will understand your self worth! Remember, you hold the keys to your destiny, no one else. You choose how you'll be treated, what will be acceptable, and those things that will not be tolerated because you have the Lover of all lovers already on your side.

Another thing that I would like for you to do is insist that the female friends and family in your life read this book. Don't give them your copy; you should keep it so that you'll have it for reference when you need it. Have them order their own copy and read it! In doing this, you will be doing your part to change the way women think all over the world. You will be changing the culture and winning souls at the same time. God said that, "he that wins souls is wise" (Proverbs 11:30). That's how we make the difference. We reach the people that are in our circle of influence and it perpetuates until everyone we know, both directly and indirectly, have been affected.

With that being said, come along with me and take a front row seat as we travel a 16-year journey filled with love, pain, and extreme amounts of God's generous mercy and grace.

I write from my knowledge, not my lack, from my strength not my weakness. I am not interested if anyone knows whether or not I am familiar with big words, I am interested in trying to render big ideas in a simple way. I am interested in being understood not admired.

-Lucille Clifton-

Before I get into my story, let's first understand who we are as women, how special we are. God said you were fearfully and wonderfully made. God took time and formed you beautifully, not to be mistreated, disrespected or abused. You are to be nurtured, loved and cared for. The man that is fortunate enough to call you his, has to appreciate you. With that appreciation comes adornment and honor, which means he doesn't talk bad to you, call you out of your name, cheat on you or make you feel **less than**. The right man will make you feel beautiful and special. He'll treat you like his queen, glad to have you by his side and not afraid to tell you. Understand your worth. Don't be afraid to be alone until Mr. Right shows up. You see, the enemy uses fear to torment people—it keeps you from receiving God's best, because when we're in fear we often make decisions without thinking them through. We're only looking at the right now, as opposed to how this decision is going to affect our future. We do this not only in relationships, but also with financial decisions, as well as other areas of our life. We will allow a man to make us feel insecure and ugly because we're afraid we won't find another man who'll treat us better and we don't want to be alone. There's nothing wrong with being alone and treating yourself like a queen until somebody else takes the job.

You see if you're used to a certain kind of treatment, then nobody can just come along with any ole' thing and you fall for those same old tricks! If I look in the mirror everyday and I think what I see is beautiful, you won't be able to come along and tell me that I'm not. If I buy myself nice clothes and treat myself to dinner, then you won't be able to come along and do nothing. If I work hard to have a nice home and a new car to drive, you can't come along and refuse to work or refuse to pay the bills if you do work, because you're spending your money in the streets. So, let's spend some time loving ourselves first, and then we'll have a greater expectation for what we'll accept from the man in our life.

For those of you who are already married stop limiting yourself. Don't be afraid to dream, assuming every time you try or want to get out of the box "oh he doesn't want to do that" (whatever "that" is). For example, something as simple as another couple asking you to go out to dinner, you want to go but you don't think he will, so you stay at home. Or you'd like to take a vacation and go somewhere nice for a couple of days, but you say to yourself "oh he wouldn't want to do that or we don't have any money for that," never being free to move forward and enjoy life. Stop being trapped in your mind and emotions, afraid to do something different. You only get one life to live down here, so you need to enjoy it to the fullest. John 10:10 in the NCV Bible says,

> *"A thief comes to steal and kill and destroy, but I came to give life — life in all its fullness."*

Jesus died for you to have the GOOD LIFE so you may as well start partaking of it. Now, this doesn't mean that with every little thing your husband does wrong, that you're going to beat him over the head with it, or take the "I ain't taking that" attitude about everything. I'm not saying that, cause then you'll end up alone and bitter or maybe yielding to a lesbian spirit, with the mindset that no man is good enough anymore. Remember, God called us to help them. That's what we do best.

If you've never taken a vacation with your husband then plan one. You may have to start with something small and work your way up. That's okay just start somewhere. If you don't have enough money to leave the city limits then go to a nice hotel in your city and pretend you're out of town. Go out to dinner and a movie or shopping and come back to the hotel. There's something about getting out of the routine and doing something different that brings excitement to your relationship. Your lovemaking will even be more exciting in a different environment. Swim in the pool or sit in the Jacuzzi, anything to shut the rest of the world out, relax and focus on each other. The more you plan these little getaways, the more he'll realize how much you all need them and he'll stop being hesitant to go. Do something special for him while you're away and he really won't mind going the next time. Whatever you do, DON'T let life pass you by.

What I'm saying to you in all of this is if women as a whole would raise their standards about what's acceptable and what's not, then men as a whole would have a greater respect for women and would step up their game. Men can only do what women allow. If women all over the world decide that they are going to keep themselves and wait on God's best, because they know they're worth it, men all around the world would change as well; they would have no choice, because they wouldn't have anybody to sleep with! The Bible says that if a man doesn't work he doesn't eat (2 Thessalonians 3:10). Now if that held true and people really didn't get to eat, then it would force them to go to work, and you wouldn't have very many lazy people, because they would starve to death. The same holds true, if men couldn't get their needs met without a marriage license, then more men would stop being playboys and get married. You force change by changing yourself.

Now let's get into my story! I pray that your life will never be the same after reading this book. You may laugh while reading this book, cry, or you may even do both! One thing I can guarantee is that this book is going to change your life in some way. May the Holy Spirit enlighten you and strengthen you to fulfill God's divine purpose for your life. Stop right now, look in the mirror and say to yourself, "I'm FABULOUS! GOD TOOK HIS TIME AND FORMED ME! NO MORE USING ME UP DEVIL, I'M WORTH WAITING FOR!"

Chapter 1
"The Calm Before The Storm"

The woman who appeals to a man's vanity may stimulate him, the woman who appeals to his heart may attract him, but it is the woman who appeals to his imagination who gets him.

-Helen Rowland-

This is how it all started: I was a 15-year-old sophomore in high school and I fell hopelessly in love with a man named Darren Brown. At the beginning of my freshmen year of high school, maybe during the first week of school, I was coming down the stairs from the third floor to the second when a voice came from my right. "Maaaan, I've got to have you!" he said. "Whatever!" I exclaimed, "I don't think so!" As the year went on, this guy would keep trying in his efforts to make me his girl, but I had no interest in him at all—I wouldn't give him the time of day. But during my sophomore year, one day as I was leaving cheerleading practice, he just happened to be waiting outside and asked if he could walk me home. For whatever the reason, that day, I said yes. It seemed like after that walk home I fell hopelessly in love with this man. He had to be the sweetest person I had ever met. He was so gentle and kind that I loved him instantly.

Needless to say, there were many walks home after that day and all I wanted was to be with Darren Brown. Being with him felt so right, I knew that I would be with him forever! As I reflect, I had no business dating at 15 because of the trouble it leads to for young men and women. At the time though, all I knew was that I was 15 and in love. Darren Brown meant everything to me. If you would have randomly flipped through a notebook of mine or stumbled across papers that belonged to me, you would be hard pressed not to find "Mrs. Tonya Patterson Brown" doodled somewhere or another. I had never felt that way about anybody before. He was at my house so much that my mother said one day, "I think you need to go home." As I mentioned before, dating only leads to sexual sin, so it really should be avoided; but that's not the point here. I was a sophomore and Darren was a senior. We started dating in December of 1980 and he graduated that following year in May of 1981. He joined the

Armed Forces and was later honorably discharged in 1983, the same year I graduated high school. I went away to school to Wichita State University, only because Darren had been stationed at Whiteman Air Force Base in Wichita. He had gone back home by the time I graduated, but I decided to go ahead to Wichita anyway to see what it was like being away from home. I stayed for a year and I came back home as well. We were still dating all of this time, but we had also seen other people as well, you know how that goes.

When I came back home to Kansas City, I began attending a local community college. I left Darren for a short period and started dating someone else. I did this a few times and for whatever the reason, he would always accept me when I came back. I left knowing that I would be back. I just wanted to have some fun because I had started dating him at such a young age. At any rate, the last time I left him to date another guy, he began dating someone else as well. One day, I was riding down the street with a girlfriend of mine and saw him standing outside the convenience store with this girl. My heart became sick and I knew I had to get him back, which I immediately set out to do.

Now, by this time I had left him multiple times when I knew how much he loved me. Everybody knew how much he loved me—you could see it. I can recall one particular break up where he even pleaded with me not to hurt him like that anymore. I heard him but I went on and let him go anyway. The funny thing was that I knew I was hurting him deeply. He was in tears and all I could think about was what I wanted to do. I knew I would be back as before and expected him to be waiting as before, but this time was different. Darren started dating this new girl and before we got back together, she had gotten pregnant. I was more than sick about it. I couldn't believe it! How could somebody else be having a baby by the man I loved so much? (I believe this was the price I had to pay for being so ruthless towards him all that time. Although we had no business being involved sexually, you still can't mistreat people and go unpunished). I wanted to have his children someday after we were married. We had talked about it on several occasions. How could he do this to me I thought (like I wasn't the one who caused it). Needless to say, when I came back this time I never left again. Suddenly I had the revelation, that he was the only man for me. Don't misconstrue what I'm saying here and start taking the blame for someone else's behavior. People have to be accountable for their own actions. I'm just simply saying in this case I was wrong.

At this point, I was really feeling bad about sleeping with Darren because I really loved God and wanted to do what was right before Him. I would leave his house sometimes at night and go home and cry "Lord I don't want to be in sin, but I love being with this man." I did this on several occasions. During this stage of my life, I was working part-time and going to school full-time, but during the summer months and on school breaks I would work fulltime hours. School had just gotten out and I was asked to work the overnight shift, which was very hard for me because I wasn't used to staying up late, certainly not all night. You see I dated Darren, but you couldn't get me to do anything else. When I was in high school my mom didn't allow me to go to clubs, and by the time I was older I didn't want to go. I never smoked, drank, gotten high, cursed, or any of that, so they called me "Miss Goody Two Shoes." But I loved being with Darren Brown. I wasn't disrespectful to my Mother, (my Father had passed away when I was 17) I didn't cause any trouble, I was basically just a good kid. But one night Darren asked me to spend the night at his house and I had never done anything like that before, so I pretended to be at work, but I had called in and spent the night with him. I felt so bad about it and I was so scared. Lo and behold I find out about four weeks later that I had gotten pregnant that night. Mind you, Darren and I had been dating off and on for 5 ½ years and I had never used birth control and had never gotten pregnant. I didn't use birth control because I felt like if I got on birth control I was giving myself permission to sin and I didn't want to be in sin, so I wouldn't take it. That may not make sense to some, but it's where my thought process was at the time. I felt like I had gotten pregnant because for the first time I willingly sinned and was deceitful about it. All the time before I felt guilty, but this time was different. Mind you, the other girl is still pregnant, about seven months by now, so I really felt bad about being pregnant by him when somebody else was already about to have his baby.

My sister Anita was the first person I told that I was pregnant besides Darren. She said to me "girl didn't you see the mistakes all of us made?" You see, all of my sisters had gotten pregnant before they were married, and after getting married ended up in divorce, all but one. I thought to myself "maybe," but nobody ever talked about sex or refraining from it at my house. It was a topic that people were almost scared to bring up, although I'm not sure why since everybody seemed to be involved in it. I had five older sisters and three older brothers and none of them educated me in the area of relationships. My mother I guess just hoped I had learned from the others, because she never said anything either. Maybe because she hadn't quite figured it out herself. My father wasn't the best example of a good husband. I grew up during the time where among other things; men thought it was okay to have a woman on the side. My father did and it shook the very core of their relationship. My mother stayed, I think initially because she loved him and wanted to stay; but over time I believe it was because she didn't think that she could make it with 10 children on her own. Besides, I'm sure that there was some insecurity there that led her to believe that she had to tolerate his behavior.

Some men still feel that way today, but you have to let them know that that's not acceptable, in your relationship. You have to be a priority to *you* in order for you to be a priority to *him*. I love me and because I love me, I'm not going to allow you to treat me any kind of way. I have standards and you have to have some too. I told my husband, "I'm not telling you what to do or what not to do, I'm only telling you what I will and will not accept. You can do whatever you want; you just can't do it with me." If you respect you then he'll respect you. If you live a life of compromise and let anything go just to keep him around, then don't expect royal treatment cause you're not going to get it. I'm a QUEEN and I know it, so I only accept royal treatment. You can call it what you want, but my husband has the utmost respect for me as I do him. He's my KING and I love him dearly. We learned over the years that the key to the royal treatment was serving one another. We came to an agreement about twenty years ago that if he would do all that he could to make me happy and I would do all that I could to make him happy, we couldn't be anything but happy. In other words we put the other person's needs and desires above/before our own. The things that other people complain about, I thoroughly enjoy doing for my husband. I don't mind at all because I love making him happy. As a result he does the same thing for me. He does all that he can to make life easy for me and I appreciate his acts of kindness towards me.

That's why I'm writing this book, so that by chance I can help somebody else make the right decisions or keep somebody from making the wrong one. Somebody reading this book now may feel trapped. You may be in a relationship that's not healthy for you. Stop now, and evaluate where you are in your life and who you're with. If it's an unhealthy relationship and you're not married, it's much easier to get out of, but if you're married then there are some things that you'll have to do in order to make this relationship a healthy one. Now you'll hear me say this more than once, if somebody is beating you, don't stick around to see how this is going to turn out. GET OUT NOW, because later might be too late! Pray for him from afar, married or not. Don't allow someone to abuse you PLEASE! Have courage, don't be afraid. Joshua 1:9 in the Amplified Bible says,

"Have not I commanded you? Be strong, vigorous, and very courageous. Be not afraid, neither be dismayed, for the Lord your God is with you wherever you go ".

I know we can end up in situations like this for a number of reasons. Sometimes it may be that our self-esteem is low, we don't think highly enough of ourselves. Maybe it's because of your past, maybe you were abused as a child or you watched your mother being abused. You may even fear for your life or the life of your children if you leave. If you're afraid for your life or if he has told you that he'll kill you if you leave, I want you to understand that there is POWER and PROTECTION in the blood of Jesus. This may sound strange to you, especially if you have never received Jesus Christ into your heart. But if this is your situation right now, this is how you can get out. Pray this prayer:

"Father, you said in John 3:16 that you loved me so much that you sent your son Jesus to die for me. Jesus I accept you into my heart right now and I also accept the protection and provision that comes with being in your family. God you said in Psalm 91:11 that you

gave your angels charge over me to guard me in all of my ways. Now as I take this bold stand to get out of this dangerous situation I'm trusting that you will lead me to safety. Isaiah 48:17 say, that you are the Lord my God who leads me in the way I should go. Forgive me for the wrong choices that I've made and I'm asking you to show me exactly where I need to go and how I need to do it so that everyone involved gets away safely. I plead the blood of Jesus over my life and the life of my children, I also pray for my husband or boyfriend that you would begin to heal him of his insecurities and draw him to you by your Spirit so that he can become the man that you would have him be. I bind the enemy and his plan of destruction for my life and the life of my children. I WILL NOT DIE BUT LIVE, AND WILL PROCLAIM WHAT THE LORD HAS DONE, in Jesus' name Amen!"

Years of abuse can sometimes leave you feeling alone and empty but Jesus can fill you up again and be your best friend.

Now back to my story. When Darren told my Mother that I was pregnant, notice I said when HE told her, because I couldn't face her, she suggested that we get married. Well, I had already decided that I wasn't going to continue this life of sin, so I told Darren, either we can get married and do this thing right or you can go on about your business, forget you ever knew me and I would go away and you'll never see me again or this baby. I meant it and it didn't matter to me which way he chose at that point. I just knew that I wasn't going to continue living in a manner that was unpleasing in the sight of God any longer. As you can see, he decided that getting married was the best choice. He didn't want to lose me, and he didn't want anyone else to have me either, so we were married in September of 1986.

We weren't self-sufficient at the time, so we lived with my Mom for the first two years trying to prepare ourselves for home ownership. Our first son by the other mother was born in July of 1986, our daughter was born in February of 1987 and I became pregnant again when my daughter was only 3 months old and gave birth to a son in March of 1988.

Now, let me briefly share with you what it was like for those first two years. I'm opening up our lives to you in hopes that you will open up your heart to the Lord, realizing that whatever your circumstance or however deep the pit, if you'll stand on the Word of God, He can and He will turn it completely around for you like He did for me.

Chapter 2

"Chaos"

There is no agony like bearing an untold story inside of you.

-Maya Angelo-

1Peter 5:8 says to control yourselves and be careful! The devil, your enemy, goes around like a roaring lion looking for someone to devour. During the 1980's and 90's a numerous amount of people around the world were being devoured by increasing affluence of drugs. I realize that we all have stories to tell, because God has brought every one of us out of some kind of pit. It may not be the same pit I'm about to describe or the same pit as somebody else you know but I'm sure you had one. Rather it was sexual sin, self-righteousness, pride, lust, backbiting, jealousy, anger or something else. Now this is how the enemy got us.

In February of 1989 we bought our first home. A very nice starter home, small but I always received compliments on how pretty and nicely decorated it was. After moving everything in the house that night Darren left and didn't come back for half the night. I knew then that I was in trouble. It wasn't another woman that I had to worry about; it was a demon straight out of hell, CRACK COCAINE! He had told me about a year prior that he had started smoking crack and that he needed some help, but now I was about to experience what that really meant. For any of you who have lived with someone using cocaine, you know it's hard for them to keep a job. If they do work, you may or may not get the money and if you leave any money lying around, it will be taken. So, for the next 3½ years, that's what I had to deal with. At the same time he was still extremely kind, did all the work around the house and took care of the kids. He did everything except pay the bills. It was like living with Dr. Jekyll & Mr. Hyde.

One person was the man I fell in love with and married and the other person was the one who was invading my life at the time. You'll recall that I told you that the reason that I fell in love with him so quickly was because he was the sweetest person I had ever met. You name something that you wanted in a husband and he had it. Literally he seemed perfect until he started smoking crack. Then I began to get cheated. The husband that I knew and loved had been taken away from me. If you didn't know that he was using cocaine, you couldn't tell it just by looking at him (unless you saw him out in the streets on one of his binges). He acted perfectly normal at home, but when he got out into 'the streets' he was a totally different person, robbing, stealing and everything else that goes along with that life style. Towards the end of his addiction, things would eventually get even crazier which we'll discuss a little later. I only share this with you because the ending is so glorious, not to make him look bad in any way.

In June of 1990, I heard about a local ministry, "Harvest Church". My sister had recently started attending and as she began talking about it, it sparked my curiosity. I wanted to go see what was happening over there. I was already in church, had been all my life and loved God with all my heart (as much as I knew him). Jesus said, "to **know** me is to **love** me", so you can only love somebody as much as you know them. At any rate, I knew I needed something more than what I was getting, so I went to visit. Darren, my Mother and I went on a Sunday night because we were at our own church that morning. I had a new experience that night. I witnessed people engage in worship, which I had never encountered before.

I was in such awe that I went home and during my prayer time I asked God how people could get caught up in worship that way. I said, "How do people worship You like that?" To me it looked as if worship was all they had on their mind. Of course, I don't know what they were really thinking, but that's what it looked like to me. It looked like their total concentration was on the Lord and I was trying to figure out how they could do that without thinking about their husband needing to be saved or their light bill needing to be paid. Because that's what I was thinking about, (my husband and the light bill), and God said to me, "Tonya, I AM WHO I AM and it has nothing to do with your circumstances." He said "some people need their husband to be saved, some people their wife, somebody needs their light bill paid, somebody else the gas bill, **everybody** needs something from Me, but it has nothing to do with who I Am. You see I **Am** the Creator of the world and I'm worthy to be worshipped no matter what!" I said, "Lord you're absolutely right, what do my circumstances have to do with Who You are, You're God rather my light bill needs to paid or not." So, I began to spend a lot of time in worship, not only with my lips, but I began to worship Him with my life, by doing those things that pleased Him, and it carried me a long way. Worship enters you into the presence of the Lord you know! So, if you need direction right now, began to worship the Lord and honor Him. It's amazing the things that you'll begin to hear Him say.

Some of you may be asking the question right now, "How do I worship? Because like you, Mrs. Tonya I've never experienced worship before." Just lift your hands, and if you're some place where you can't lift your hands right now, that's okay. Just begin to tell God how much you love Him and thank Him for being so good to you. Call Him your Master, your Savior, your Counselor your Lord, your Provider, your Healer, your Deliverer, your Peace, your Joy and your Friend. There are many Biblical names that you could call Him, but until you've learned them all just call Him whatever you need Him to be in your life right now. The key is to center in completely on Jesus. Just think about if your husband or your child came to you telling you how much they loved and adored you and appreciated you being in their life, what that would mean to you. It makes you want to bless them doesn't it? It makes you want to do something kind for them. You want to make them happy. Well, that's how God is towards us when we are continuously telling Him all of these good things about Himself. It makes Him want to bless us. Really, it just opens us up to the blessings that He has already provided.

Anyway, I continued visiting when I didn't have to work on Sunday nights and eventually I had gotten to a point where I couldn't stand not to be there. So I started going on Sunday mornings. I mention this only because what I learned that next year changed our lives forever! My Mother didn't come back because she was a faithful member of her church and had no intentions on leaving. Darren would come, not all the time but sometimes and every time that he did I would be praying that somehow this day would be his day of deliverance, but it never was. When I first started going on Sunday mornings the

Pastor gave an altar call. For those of you who don't know what an altar call is, it's when the person ministering gives an invitation for people to come to the altar and accept Christ into their lives or receive prayer for something whether healing, deliverance, etc. You can have altar calls for many different things. This particular altar call was for accepting Christ, and a young man answered the altar call by going down to the front of the church. Our Pastor began to talk to the young man only to find out that he had an addiction to crack cocaine. Our Pastor laid hands on him, took authority over the addiction and **commanded** him to be free.

I had never seen anything like this before. I had never seen anybody laying hands on people exercising authority in the spirit realm. I didn't even know anything about the spirit world at this time. What I did know was that my husband was addicted to crack cocaine as well, and if God could set this man free, then my husband could be free also. I watched for this young man every week to see if he would show up at church, to see if his life was really changing. I knew if he was coming to church faithfully that he truly had been delivered because being addicted to cocaine, you can't be faithful to **anything,** not for long anyway. But he came faithfully and began to volunteer in the ministry and later was married to a young lady at the church. They're still married today. Now did he ever have any slip ups, I don't know. I never asked him, as a matter of fact, I never told anyone until now, that I was even watching him, but I watched him from afar for several years. Their family doesn't attend our church anymore, but I still see them from time to time and it serves as a reminder to me of God's power to deliver! That was way back in 1990 or 91' and I have never forgotten it.

Pastor Steve Houpe was teaching the Word in such a way that my life began to change immediately. I spent the next year or so being taught the Word of God. I was so hungry for the Word, so hungry for a change in the lives of my family and myself that I began studying the scriptures and praying daily. I wanted to get to know God better so I could know how to live my life better. As I spent time with God daily, He began to speak to me and show me things. I started to find out who I was in Christ and the authority that I had in Him. I learned how to apply the scriptures to my daily life and became a powerful tool in the hands of God that He could use to help other people as well. **My life would never be the same.**

For the next two years I was at church faithfully allowing the Word of God to renew my mind (change the way I thought). During this time God began to reveal to me how much authority I had in Him. I was praying and studying the Word daily, because I so desperately needed my situation to change. I remember one church service Pastor Houpe was ministering on the authority we have in Christ. I don't recall everything he said that day, but whatever it was it ignited a fire on the inside of me. I came home that day and said, "**ENOUGH IS ENOUGH** devil, I'm drawing the line in the sand today. You won't take another dime from me. You won't steal anymore money, from me or anybody else around me, take any more clothes or take another thing from this house in JESUS' Name!"

See, by this time I had been praying for my husband and instead of getting better, it appeared that he was getting worse (much worse). Whereas, he had been getting high, now he was getting HIGH! He would stay gone now for two to three days at a time, and would even take newly purchased clothes back to the store for money. The last time he stayed gone, he was gone for 3 weeks. At first I didn't even know whether he was dead or alive. He eventually called (this was right before he stopped smoking cocaine) and came back home. He had a lot to say about how many times he had almost gotten killed during that 3-week period and by now he was tired of that lifestyle. All the while, God was leading me by His Spirit. That's the only way I could've kept my sanity and stayed at the same time, otherwise I would've had to leave him to stay sane. That doesn't mean that there weren't days that this wasn't taking a toll on me. I'm human and I hurt just like the next person. There were many days that I felt I would crack under the pressure, but I didn't.

During this period it got really rough for me, I remember time and time again Darren would leave in the middle of the night. He would take the car and leave me with no way to get to work, or he would have the car and leave me at work with no way to get home. He would come back hours later with some story about what happened, the same as he would about his checks when he worked. You see he was a hard worker when he worked, but after he got his paycheck he would go get high and miss work, so he couldn't keep a steady job. As far as him taking the car and sometimes leaving me stranded, I think that made me angrier than anything else. I would sleep on my stomach with the keys in my bra to keep him from leaving but sometimes he would manage to get the keys anyway. That frustrated me so much that I would ask God why He would allow him to sneak the keys without me waking up. I would wake up and he would be pulling out of the driveway. I wanted to scream I would be so angry. I would tell God "all You had to do was wake me up a few minutes earlier, why do You keep letting him do this to me?" I don't think I blamed God for anything else, but when it came to this, I felt like He could have awakened me and prevented this. So for those of you in the middle of a similar situation right now, I know how you feel. The enemy wants to get us angry with God, because if he can get us angry and blaming God for what's wrong, then we won't be exercising our faith in God to change the situation and he wins. You see, faith works by love and if you're not operating in the love walk, your faith can't work. It got really rough towards the end, but that was the enemy's plot to get me to give up. Remember that as you start to speak the Word over your situation, the enemy will always turn up the heat to get you to say forget it, this isn't working or it's never going to change. Don't **ever** yield to those thoughts, its working; you just keep speaking the Word and believing God. He'll bring about the change you desire because the word of God never fails. There were numerous other incidents that happened during this season, you can only imagine. But just like I'm telling you, I didn't quit.

Despite all of that, I knew that God had a plan for him, that's the only reason I stayed. I remember being at my cousins wedding one day. Darren didn't come with me; it was just my Mother and I. One of my cousins asked me where Darren was and I said he didn't come. He walked away laughing and mumbling something about he was probably somewhere smoking crack. He was trying to be funny, but it really hurt my feelings. I don't really remember what I said to him, but I told him he didn't have any business saying anything about my husband. Later that night I asked God "why everybody was talking about Darren?" It seemed as though our entire family had something to say about him at the time. Nobody was even around my husband enough to know these things about him, so it was clear that he had to be the topic of a lot of conversations. I said "we don't talk about anybody and we know things about a lot of our family members, but we don't say anything so why is everybody running him in the ground?" God said to me that day, "Tonya for what I'm going to do in Darren's life, everybody has to see **this** side in order to know the awesomeness of what I'm going to do later. You see if they don't see **this** side of him, then they won't be able to appreciate the miracle that is his life later." I said, "oh okay, you have a plan in all of this, well let them talk then." From that day forward I no longer worried about what people said about him, because I knew God had a plan for his life. My job in God's master plan was to pray, speak the Word and believe!

One day as I was reading my Bible during my normal study time, I began to read Mark 9. This chapter was about a man who was bringing his son to Jesus for healing from demons that took control of his body. After realizing that Jesus wasn't there, the man asked Jesus' disciples to cast the demon out. The disciples had no success with the young boy. When Jesus walked up He asked, "What are you arguing with them about?"

> 17 *A man in the crowd answered, "Teacher, I brought you my son, who is possessed by a spirit that has robbed him of speech. 18 Whenever it seizes him, it throws him to the ground. He foams at the mouth, gnashes his teeth and becomes rigid. I asked your disciples to drive out the spirit, but they could not." 19 "You unbelieving generation," Jesus replied, "How long shall I stay with you? How long shall I put up with you? Bring the boy to me." 20 So they brought him. When the spirit saw Jesus, it immediately threw the boy into a convulsion. He fell to the ground and rolled around, foaming at the mouth. 21 Jesus asked the boy's father, "How long has he been like this?" "From childhood," he answered. 22 "It has often thrown him into fire or water to kill him. But if you can do anything, take pity on us and help us." 23 "'If you can'?" said Jesus. "Everything is possible for one who believes." 24*

Immediately the boy's father exclaimed, "I do believe; help me overcome my unbelief!" 25 When Jesus saw that a crowd was running to the scene, he rebuked the impure spirit. "You deaf and mute spirit," he said, "I command you, come out of him and never enter him again." 26 The spirit shrieked, convulsed him violently and came out. The boy looked so much like a corpse that many said, "He's dead." 27 But Jesus took him by the hand and lifted him to his feet, and he stood up

(Mark 9:17-27 NIV).

When the Bible says he began to shriek and jerk and go into convulsions, I could see the demon like a small child throwing a temper tantrum on the floor, kicking, screaming and bumping his head against the ground. At that moment I heard the Holy Spirit say to me, "that's what's going on in Darren's life right now, the enemy is shrieking and jerking and going into convulsions because he doesn't want to let him go. So in the natural, it looks like all hell has broken loose because in the spirit realm, the devil's having a fit." "Oh is that right?" I said with a sigh of relief. "Well I'll tell you what, you can kick, scream and have a fit all you want to, right on back to hell where you came from, cause this man right here belongs to JESUS! You can't have him!"

I had many days like that dealing with these spirits because they were stubborn and didn't want to leave. But I knew there was power in the name of Jesus and I wasn't taking no for an answer.

Have you ever been physically slapped in the face? I haven't, but spiritually I've been slapped a few times. I was reading Luke 10:18-19, which states in the KJV,

> *"18 And he said unto them, I beheld Satan as lightning fall from heaven. 19 Behold, I give unto you power to tread on serpents and scorpions, and over all the power of the enemy: and nothing shall by any means hurt you. "*

It was like He slapped me in the face and said, "look Tonya, you are not just reading words on a piece of paper, I'm telling you where he is, I saw him with my own eyes **fall** like lightning from heaven. I have given you power over him, now **exercise your authority!**" I said, "you mean I've just been getting my behind whooped all this time for nothing?" You see, the authority he spoke of wasn't just for Darren's freedom but for every area of my life. So with the same authority I used to get victory in that area of our lives, I also used to bring us out of poverty and lack. God doesn't desire for you to be poor, sick or bound by the enemy in any way.

Darren *had* to be free it wasn't optional for me. So, I pressed in more and more every day until the day I just told you about, when I came home and said, "ENOUGH IS ENOUGH!" That day I wasn't taking anymore. I knew it, God knew it and the devil knew it, and it stopped **instantly**. No more stealing, no more running off with the car leaving me stranded. NO MORE smoking crack. All of it stopped, just like that. He said he just woke up one morning and decided that he didn't want to smoke anymore. "I bet you did," I said (smile) He had no idea of the spiritual warfare that had been going on.

I remember one day, God told me to anoint him with oil while he was asleep. I said, "Lord I

can't do that, he'll wake up wondering what I'm
doing," but God said, "no, anoint him," so I did. I
anointed his feet to only go places God would
have him go and his hands to only do those things
God would have him do, and his head so that he
would only think thoughts God would have him
think. I prayed for him that night and anointed
him with oil. There was such a sweet presence of
the Lord in that room when I got done. He never
moved and slept like a baby for the rest of the
night. This may sound strange to some people.
This is not witchcraft or some kind of crazy ritual,
but the power of prayer and faith. Many times
God would tell me what to do to bring us out of
this situation. The key ladies, is to be led by the
Spirit, the Holy Spirit that is. He knows all things,
so He knows exactly how to bring you out of any
situation. God's not spooky, as some would say, or
strange either. He's none of those things; He was
simply showing me that He alone was all-powerful
and that the enemy had no power that could
stand against the blood of Jesus.

One day as I was praying, I don't know why
I saw it this way, but as I was pleading the blood
of Jesus over my situation, I envisioned Satan
backing down like I was holding a cross up to a

vampire. He had no power to stand against the blood of Jesus! The more I plead the blood, the lower he got to the ground covering his face because he couldn't take it. Remember the greater one is in **you.** You have the greater power, not the devil (1John 4:4). That's what kept Darren alive all those years in the "streets". It was the power of prayer. I was also pleading the blood of Jesus over his life every day for protection because I knew the enemy was trying to kill him. Had it not been for the grace of God he surely would've been dead.

As I stated earlier, Darren abruptly stopped smoking cocaine...But, guess what? He then started *selling* it. You're talking about going from bad to worse. "He must really be crazy now," I thought. He went from the lowest pit, to walking around like Al Pacino in *"The Godfather,"* his chest stuck out, head big, and a pocket full of money. He really thought he had it going on because now he was making money. I didn't want the money. I didn't want anything to do with that lifestyle. Let me say this to those of you whose husband, boyfriend or son is caught up in a life of selling drugs. Don't tell him to give up that lifestyle, yet turn around and spend the money that his lifestyle is bringing in. The more that you partake of what drug money provides the harder it is for them to give it up. They feel like they're providing for you and they can't afford to give you that kind of life otherwise, so they use that as an excuse to keep selling. That's just deception to keep them in the game.

You see, the enemy desires to destroy them by either getting them killed, or by sending them to prison. That's where the drug life leads you. There aren't many other options. That's why I never took the money. I didn't want him to feel like he was providing something for us that he couldn't let go of. I soon told him he had to leave our home if that's what he was going to do because I didn't want our kids to be in harm's way. He promised he would never put his children in any danger or expose them to that life, which up to that point he hadn't. But I didn't want something to go wrong or for somebody to come looking for him at our house. So, he began staying at the "dope" house. When I needed him for something I would go over there, honk the horn and he would come out to the car. Soon after, I began to ride by there on occasion, stretching my hands toward the house commanding it to close in Jesus' name, that house and any other house he may have been involved in at the time. It was just a matter of a few short months before there was a drug bust and he along with the rest of his co-defendants were arrested and all the drug houses that they were involved with were closed! The only problem was that now he was in jail. I said "Lord I wasn't specific, I said close them, I didn't mean for him to get arrested in the process." (**That's the power of words!**)

Words are powerful, so make sure that when you're confessing, that you are being specific about what it is that you want. That was a very valuable lesson for me. The words that you speak have the power to produce death and life, so be careful what you say. Read Proverbs 18:21. When he called to tell me he had been arrested I didn't even care at first. I thought it was just another ploy, a game he was playing. Soon I realized that this was no game and that he was looking at doing some serious time. He was arrested in July of 1992. The court appointed him an attorney because he didn't have any money to hire one. Whatever money he made I didn't take, so if he had any it was stolen during or after the bust. The attorney first told us that he was looking at about five years. I remember thinking to myself "there is absolutely no way my husband is doing five years in prison." Then the five years turned into 40! They were trying to give him 40 years for a few short months of selling drugs. I knew people who had been to jail several times and had never gotten any real time, so I couldn't understand how they could be talking about 40 years. I began to pray, that's all I knew to do.

About this time we were trying to see if we could get him out on bond. The attorney came to me and said his bond was set at $25,000 and I needed $2,500 to get him out. Well, I didn't have $2,500, so once again I began to pray. Then one morning I was on my way to work praying like I usually did, and something (the Holy Spirit) rose up in me and I began to take authority over the situation. I bound the devil and told the Holy Spirit to deal with the heart of this judge (I called her by name). Don't let her rest until she let's my husband go. Proverbs 21:1 in the NCV says,

> *"The Lord can control a king's mind as he controls a river, he can direct it as he pleases".*

So I was simply asking God to give Darren favor with the king, which in this case was the judge. About an hour or two after I had gotten to work, I received a phone call. A gentleman stated his name and said he was calling to see if I had any amount of money that I could use for bond. He said he didn't know what happened, but that the judge did a 360. She wanted to let him go, and she just wants to know if anybody believed enough in him that they would be willing to put up any amount of money. I responded, "Yes sir, I have $500." He said, "okay, we go before the judge in a couple of days, I'll see if she'll take it." She did and he was home before the week was out, **HALLELUJAH!**

This was October 30, 1992 and by the first of December I was pregnant with our youngest daughter. I couldn't believe it! I was so upset because I didn't feel that this was the right time to have another baby. I proclaimed! "Lord I told you not now!" (like I was the one in control). I didn't know that he would be going back to jail before the baby was born and that this baby would be what carried me through, **but God did.**

Darren was out on bond from October of 1992 until May of 1993 and during that time I never saw any real change in him concerning his relationship with Christ. I could tell that he was nervous about the time that he was facing, and it seemed like he was trying to get into everything he could before he left. I understand that now because I think about what he must have been going through mentally, facing that long sentence. At that time, however, all I could think about was what about me and our children, what are we going to do? I know it's hard to have sympathy for someone who seems to keep making the same mistakes over and over. You're probably thinking that, "if you had just listened in the first place, none of this would be happening, so NO! I don't feel sorry for you." I understand how you feel because I felt the same way.

I had a friend whose husband was out on bond and facing ten years. It didn't appear to her that she was his main concern, and knowing that he was about to be gone for 10 years, she left him. She couldn't understand why during this period that he wasn't spending more time cultivating their relationship. But men are different than women, we think about situations differently.

He's not acting like that because he doesn't care, he's just afraid of what he's about to face and doesn't know how to relate that to you for you to help him. He may also feel like he's disappointed you for even being in this situation, because of course, he didn't think he would get caught. So he's feeling some embarrassment and shame right now along with the fear. He certainly does not want to admit to you that he's afraid. In my friends case what her husband didn't know was that if he had only spent that time showing some remorse for his actions and proving to her how much he loved and needed her, she would have waited the ten years. But even after going through all of the other suffering he still showed no appreciation all the way to the end. So when he finally reported in for custody, she decided that he wasn't worth waiting for. Some of you reading this book now, feel the same way and if you're not married I would say to you don't waste your time waiting. If he's not treating you right now, what are you waiting for? If you're married, pray and let the Holy Spirit lead you. One thing about men in prison is that they don't want to be alone. You may find yourself being used by someone, because it's convenient for them. They need somebody to talk to, someone to put money on their books and somebody to have phone sex with. Usually they straighten their game up during their confinement, because their resources are limited. But after they get released from prison, a lot of men start to explore their other options with no regard for the time that they've taken from you. So, be cautious.

Men have a tendency to keep this wall up never allowing you to be apart of all of them. What they don't realize is you'll love them in and through all of their deficiencies and shortcomings if they'll just be open and honest. You were created by God to help them, what they have to do is let you! Secrets only bring distance to your relationship, keeping it real will bring you closer together. Love done right is a beautiful thing.

Now back to my story. One Sunday morning Darren decided that he was going to church with us. He went to church off and on, but not consistently. This particular Sunday I didn't want him to go. I had never, NOT wanted him to go, as a matter of fact, that's what I wanted him to do more than anything else. I recall one day I was so angry that he wouldn't get up to go to church with us, that I threw the phone and hit him with it while he was still lying in bed. He threw it back, but he made sure that he didn't hit me with it. He said he only wanted to scare me. I thought to myself that day, I wonder, what if he had hit me in the head with that phone. I could've been dead right there on the steps and everybody would've blamed him for it not knowing that I had been hitting him all the time without him ever hitting me back. My Mom would often say to me, "Stop hitting on him all the time. You know that he's being king and won't fight you back, so leave him alone." So I decided **that** day that I wasn't going to hit him anymore. Deliverance can come at any time and in all kinds of ways. That was my day of deliverance I never hit him again. Anyway, that day I felt like he was only trying to get on my good side by going, and I wasn't in the mood for any more games. At any rate, even though I asked him not to, he went to church anyway and boy was I glad he did. He answered the altar call that day and gave his life to Christ. He was also filled with the Holy Spirit that day with the evidence of speaking in other tongues (Read Acts 2).

Darren had gotten saved that day, but he needed time to have his mind renewed. He needed to be taught the Word of God so that he could change the way he thought. Three weeks later, Darren was asked to report to the courthouse to be taken back into custody. I was devastated but I realized that God had filled him with His Spirit just in time. He knew that Darren was getting ready to go back even though we didn't, so he was preparing him for the journey. One thing that I noticed immediately was the sense of inner peace on him this time, that he didn't have the first time. When he was first arrested, he was in a panicked state of mind. He probably felt like he was going to break under the pressure. I can only imagine how that must have felt to him. He was very uneasy, not sure of his fate. This time, even though he did not want to go back, he felt like he could, almost like he had the strength to. Now he was still a "babe" in Christ, so he didn't by any means have it all together, and he made plenty of mistakes along the way. Eventually he had another encounter with God while he was in the hole in one of the maximum-security prisons. An experience he talks about in his book "BUG: Straight Talk, the story of *a man's life, his 16 year journey through prison and the woman who waited*." After that experience he really started spending time developing his relationship with Christ. He read and studied the Word of God, and spent an abundant time in prayer causing his life to change drastically.

I had a friend call and ask me one day, she said "Brown, I saw how Darren's life changed and how you stood on the Wand didn't quit, now tell me how you did it? What scriptures did you use? Tell me what kinds of confessions you were making. I'm going to write it down so that I can do the same thing. My husband is on drugs and I didn't know it at the time when you were telling me about Darren, so tell me now what I need to do." I said "Okay, but let me warn you first that when you start praying like I was praying and confessing scriptures like I was doing, the enemy is going to turn up the heat! He knows the only way that you won't get what you believe God for is if you quit, so he'll try to attack you in all kinds of ways to get you to give up. Otherwise you can have what you say. But don't be moved by that, *just be aware*. God has already given you the VICTORY you just have to take it."

I remember one day I could hear in the spirit the devil telling his demons to "shut me up!" He said, "shut her up, because if you don't shut her up we're going to lose him" (Darren). Darren told me later after all of this was over that he could see why the devil didn't want to lose him, because he was one of his best employees. Thank God he was leading me by his Spirit through his Word. That was what enabled me to stand, I was standing in His (God) strength, not my own. I was saying things like "Lord I thank you that Darren loves you with all of his heart, soul, mind and strength. And he loves me as Christ loves the church and gave Himself for it. His eyes are only for me, no other woman can satisfy him neither do they interest him. I would also include him in scriptures, saying things like Darren; God has delivered you from the power of darkness and hath translated you into the kingdom of his dear Son (Colossians 1:13). Romans 4:17 says that,

> *"God is a God that gives life to the dead and calls things that be not as though they were."*

So I was speaking over him what God said about him, not those things that I saw with my eyes. I probably had about ten or fifteen scriptures that I spoke over him daily if not more. I had never been so persistent about anything before in my life.

Anyway, my friend called me back maybe a few weeks later and said "Brown I'm through with that, that's your testimony! Girl it seemed like stuff was coming up out of the ground against my family and me. I was already dealing with enough, I couldn't take anymore!" I tried to convince her not to quit, but she couldn't see past her current situation enough to believe God that it would change. Shortly thereafter, she filed for a divorce, which is exactly what the devil wanted. He hates marriage and he hates you, not because you're you but because of what you stand for. He hates Jesus, that's why he attacks those who serve Him. But remember, you have the greater power! (1 John 4:4). She regrets that decision today. She often tells me that she wishes she had stood on the Word and believed God, especially after seeing the outcome of me and Darren's relationship. Plus, she says going through that divorce was very hard on her children. She only wishes that she could have been more persistent. One very important thing I've noticed is that if you don't believe God in one area, you'll have to believe Him in another. At some point you'll have to learn how to persevere and not give up.

You tell God what kind of man you want and then God gives him to you but in seed form (as in, a seed that has to be planted and watered before it grows). You're thinking, God this isn't what I asked you for and God is saying yes it is, but he needs your help. That's why I've given you to him, to help him. Some of the gifts and abilities that are in men never reach their full potential until you, his help mate, come along to help him shine. Read Proverbs 31. Of course some men need more help than others and when you're with the right person; all that he needs is in you.

Chapter 3

My Imprisonment:

Don't I Have A Choice?

The situations that will stretch your faith most will be those times when life falls apart and God seems nowhere to be found. Think of Job who lost everything in one day and for 37 chapters, God said nothing. When chaos is all around and you can't see because of the tears in your eyes, these are the times when you have to hope against all hope.

-Darren Brown-

I was in prison and didn't even know it. I would have to spend the next 15 years of my life not locked behind bars, but not free to enjoy male companionship or adult outings or experiences that I desired and could only do with him. When I was 7 months pregnant Darren was sentenced to 15 years in a federal prison. I thought my life was over. I had no idea how I would bear this, but I quickly learned that God's grace was more than sufficient. This wasn't a week-by-week, month-by month or year-by-year ordeal. It was truly a day-by-day walk. I had no idea how I was going to do this time with him. I didn't make it until I made it! I didn't have a recipe for how this was supposed to work. I can recall one afternoon after I had already received the news of his sentencing; I was on my way to see him but had stopped at the store to get a few things for our trip. As I was standing in line waiting to pay for my groceries, I passed out. I fainted right there at the checkout counter! I was completely overwhelmed at the time, stressing and anxious, because I really had no idea how I was supposed to handle this. There were no books dealing with this situation for me to read. I had to figure it out, day-by-day and night-by-night. Even though a person is not doing all that they should, you can become dependent on the things that they do. For several years I was dealing with this drug use and distribution, but in spite of all that, I still depended on him for a lot of things. He still represented some form of security for me. That's why it was so hard for me to accept the fact that he would no longer physically be there for our kids and me. I never wanted to be without him, I only wanted him to be free.

It appeared that I had become "one of them." It seemed as though our family was going to be another statistic. Another African American man behind bars and a wife and four children left with no father. I'm sure that some expected that we would end up poor, on welfare and that our kids would probably end up as teenage dropouts or in prison themselves. Thank God though, for His amazing grace!

When I first went to see him, he was in a holding facility where you had to talk to him on the phone through a thick Plexiglas. That was a heart wrenching experience. You're scared, nervous, and you don't know what to expect. Pulling onto the grounds alone can be scary. There were several men with guns standing on guard, cameras at every angle, barbed wire fencing nearly 20 feet high, and somebody watching you at all times. You don't feel protected and safe, you feel like a criminal as well. It was demeaning for me and for our children. So I could only imagine what he must have been feeling. I was looking at all of the other families that were there visiting as well. I wasn't alone by any means. There were other wives, girlfriends, mothers, fathers, sisters, brothers and children there visiting also that day and I thought to myself, 'Lord what in the world have we gotten ourselves into?' Not to mention the fact that the visits only lasted 30 minutes, sometimes an hour in those kind of facilities. I can't describe the feeling the first time I visited. I watched him walk back behind that wall, out of my view, beyond my touch and out of my world. It was devastating and the thing about it was, it never got better for me. It always made me sad to see him walk away. When we went to court for the initial charges they brought him in chained hand and foot like an animal. I almost wanted to scream. To see my husband, the man I loved so much handled like property, to just a number—06998-045 was his— was horrible. There was one facility that he was sent to that literally felt like a dungeon. It felt very cold and lifeless. It made me feel creepy just walking inside of it. I told him during my first visit there that I would never comeback. So I didn't see him for nearly six months when he was able to transfer to another facility.

It was during the first year of his imprisonment that I realized what being a single parent was all about. I stated earlier, how I couldn't count on getting any money from him unless I got it before he got to the streets. Other than that, he did everything else. He never wanted me to do any work around the house, but he loved it when I cooked, even though he did the majority of that as well. I remember the first time I told him I was cutting the grass and the pain he felt on the other end. He was so hurt behind it that he still talks about it to this day. Not only was I cutting grass now, but I had to wash my own car, clean the house, cook, wash clothes, take care of the kids, be at all of the football games, dance recitals, and parent teacher conferences, on top of having to work full-time as the sole provider.

I also realized during this first year just how many of our men are locked behind bars. Seeing all of those families come to visit made me realize that these were people just like we were. I guess subconsciously I had only imagined prisons being full of these cruel crazy people who didn't deserve to be a part of society. But the reality of what I saw, were men who in fact loved their children and children who loved their fathers like mine did. There were mothers and fathers visiting their sons, sisters visiting their brothers, girlfriends visiting their boyfriends or wives visiting their husbands. Some men are cruel and deserve to be in prison, but a lot of these men are people just like you and I, who simply made mistakes that, changed their lives forever. I soon began to realize as well that these prisons were a form of genocide for African-American males and therefore the African-American community as a whole. By taking our men away, women are being robbed of the security of having male protection, provision, and companionship and the children are being robbed of the protection, provision and guidance of their father and left with no positive role models. These factors create crime, violence, poverty, high dropout rates and numerous other things because our men are the foundation of our families. Without them the family suffers.

Darren spent the first four years in Springfield after he was sentenced. Springfield was only two and a half hours from Kansas City, so I was able to see him every other weekend, which was the most that they would allow. If they had let me go every weekend I would have. That was simply the grace of God, because initially I couldn't afford spending a lot of money traveling to different places to see him. I would have, but we wouldn't have gotten to see him as often. So I was very grateful during this season. Besides, I had 3 young children, two of which were in school, so the weekends were all we had. We made the most of our trips. I tried to do all that I could to provide the best life for my children. I didn't want them to feel cheated somehow because of the situation they were in. So every other weekend we got up early on Saturday morning and headed for Springfield, Missouri. Visiting hours began at 8 or 8:30am and I always wanted to be there as soon as they started so that we would have the whole day together. After the visits, which ended promptly at 3:00pm, we would always go shopping at the mall and out to dinner. Sometimes we would go to places like Chuck E. Cheese. I don't think they had an actual Chuck E. Cheese, but places like that, with the arcade style video games, pizza and go-karts that my children loved.

We would go to furniture stores and even go look at new homes. We were always planning to have more than what we had. So for them, going to see Daddy was an adventure. It was like being on vacation every other week, well at least until they were teenagers. Sometimes we drove down to Branson and went to the amusement park, or went to play miniature golf, just whatever I could find for them to do to enjoy living. Just because we were in this situation didn't mean that we would be defeated by it. Eventually when they moved him to other facilities going to see him would become a vacation. We visited places that we probably otherwise wouldn't have gone to and we enjoyed the city while we were there. But after all the shopping, sightseeing and running the kids around, when we got back to the hotel and the kids were down for bed, I was left alone with my thoughts. And they were always, "Lord how long can I do this?"

I hurt for my children. I think that was the part about him being gone that hurt the most. When I received that letter that said he had been sentenced to 15 years, I nearly passed out, I couldn't believe it. The first thing I said was, "Lord what are we going to do in 15 years, our life will be over by then, my kids will have graduated high school and he will have missed everything, he won't be there for them at all." That was a pain that I can't describe, because I just didn't want them to have to suffer through that. He was not going to be at any parent teacher conferences, our son's football and basketball games, or even to take our daughters on their first date. There were so many things that I had planned for my children and now it appeared that it had all been ruined. I also didn't want people looking at my children like they had an absentee father by choice, in other words, a father who could've been there but chose not to, because they didn't. I wanted people to know that my children were loved and cared for by their father. It was a shame that I didn't want them to carry.

I had never thought about it before, but I guess in a situation like this, you start to take the blame for some of it. After all, I did marry him. If I had made the right choice, then my children wouldn't be suffering like this. But how was I to know that saying yes to that walk home all of those years ago, was going to end me up with three children and a father in prison. That's a tough pill to swallow, a very harsh truth staring you in the face. The decisions you make do impact your life and often times your family, which is why it's so important to be led by the Spirit. If you're feeling that way now, if you're blaming yourself or you're stuck in self pity, the best thing that you can do for you and your children is to FORGIVE yourself, forgive him and keep it moving. Even if you're not with him anymore, make sure you forgive him. You can't change the past. There's no one living who hasn't made some decisions that they regret. The key is to realize when you've made a mistake so that you don't make the same one again, and that you learn all that you can from it.

Lastly, ask God to bring something good out of your mistakes. In every situation, it's all in the way you handle it that determines rather the impact will be good or bad. I decided that in spite of our bad choices that I was going to make the most of what we had to deal with. I'm not saying that marrying him was a bad decision because that's a decision that I would never change even if I had my life to live over again. I believe that we truly are soul mates and I don't want to be with anyone else. But, I also believe that there was decisions that we both made that led us down the path that we were on; some of which weren't good, obviously.

We used up all of our visiting hours every month because I wanted to make sure that our children could see their father and talk to him as much as possible. I made sure they had the best of everything, maybe overcompensating I'm not sure, but I didn't want them to feel ashamed. We as parents felt enough of that for them. Eventually those feelings of shame and guilt went away. I realized that life sometimes brings challenges that you never expected, but because God is faithful, He always enables you not only to go through those challenges, but to come out on TOP! Sometimes God brings you so far up, that people would never believe that you were ever at the bottom.

My life was completely engrossed with these three children he left me with. I made them my priority and as I shared with you earlier he had another child, his first-born son before we were married. I admit it; I had a hard time accepting him. For the first several years, I didn't allow Darren to really communicate with him like he wanted or even should have. And he certainly couldn't bring him over to our house. That was really hard on my husband, but I felt like his son's mother still wanted to be with him and I just didn't want anything to do with the situation. I'm sure many of you can attest to that. But one day at church, during the time I was pregnant with our youngest daughter, which means, Darren hadn't been gone very long, they had a one-day marriage seminar for the married couples of the church. I decided to attend even though Darren was away. They were having a question and answer session. You would write down your questions anonymously and pass them to the front. The Pastor would read the questions and then he or his wife would give the answer. Well, somebody asked the question, "How do you know when you have forgiven?" and the answer was given "When the hurt doesn't hurt anymore!" **OH MY GOD!** Those words pierced my heart. Just the thought of someone else having his child felt like somebody was sticking a knife into my back and turning it, it hurt so bad. I went home and I cried out to the Lord that night, "God please forgive me!" I had no idea that I was holding un-forgiveness in my heart it just hurt so badly. I knew enough of the Word to know that if I didn't forgive others, God couldn't forgive me (Mark 11:25-26 KJV) and the last thing I wanted was to not be in right fellowship with the Lord. So I wrote Darren a letter that night, apologizing to him, asking him to forgive me and freeing him to see his son and to be the father that he so desperately desired to be. It was like something lifted off of our relationship. We instantly began to grow closer and became a much stronger unit. We were becoming **one**, not physically, but emotionally and spiritually, we were becoming of one mind, developing unity. We were finally walking together. The knife had been removed from my back and eventually his son would come to live with us. He's all grown up now with a beautiful family of his own, and I love him just as if I had bore him myself. That's how much God can turn things around, but only if you let Him.

None of this was any reflection on her, I would've felt that way whoever she was, the purpose of me sharing this is to show the condition of my heart and how God healed and changed **me.** I only share it because I know so many of you can relate to this. Probably 70-80% of women have to guard their hearts from offense when it comes to another child's mother depending on the circumstances under which the child was conceived. But don't hold it, it only hurts you and hinders your progress. Be the bigger person and walk in love. It takes a much stronger person to walk in love and forgiveness than it does to hold anger and un-forgiveness. Remember the other woman is not thinking about what this issue has done to you. They're only considering themselves and their baby, not your reaction to it!

Chapter 4

Has He Really Changed?

I, just like you, had heard many stories about people going to prison and pretending they had changed or had what they call "jail-house" religion, which is acting religious while they're in prison but when they get out they go right back to their old ways. Well, I needed to know the difference. I needed to know if what I was seeing and hearing was real. I cried many days for God to bring Darren home early but there were also many days that I would say, "God I don't care how much I cry and beg, don't release him from this place until this thing is settled." I'd rather be crying through this part then have him come home unchanged and end up in divorce court. Because I knew the person that I had become couldn't tolerate the person he used to be anymore and I didn't want to be without him. So I would rather suffer now then despise him later.

As time went on, Darren met some good Christian men that God used to disciple him. His life was changing so drastically that I could hardly believe it (**Don't fool yourself; there are a lot of good men in prison**). But don't misinterpret what I'm saying either. That doesn't mean that YOUR man is in prison, I'm just saying don't always count them out. If you do decide to give one a chance, allow him time to get readjusted to society and time to heal before getting involved with him. Otherwise you'll probably have a lot of challenges that you're not prepared to deal with.

One day I received an envelope in the mail with money inside and a note that stated, "Hi my name is _____, I was incarcerated with your husband and was just recently released. Would you please buy something for your children and tell them that it's from their Dad, because he loves you and his children so much that I just wanted to do something for them." On visits men would come up to me and tell me what a blessing Darren had been to them and how blessed they were to know him. I couldn't believe it. I couldn't believe the kind of impact that he was having on other people's lives. So I would ask God often, "Was this real, had he really changed?" God would reply different times, but this particular time God said, "Tonya, at some point you're going to have to believe that you have received what you've been praying for. You know a tree by the fruit it bears, what kind of fruit is he bearing?" I said, "I see the fruit, but I want to know if the fruit is real." The reality was that I hadn't seen anybody change so drastically, so fast. Not even in the church.

One day I found myself sitting and thinking about some incidents from years prior to this point that I had never gotten the truth about, but now wanted to know. I can't even remember now what the incidents were, because truth of the matter, they weren't important. The important thing was that God was showing me that I could trust Darren again. He was strengthening our relationship and this was one of the ways He used to do so. I told God that I wanted to know the truth about these things that happened years earlier. I said, "God I won't be angry or act ugly, or any of that, I just want to know because I never knew the truth." About two days later I get a letter in the mail and **everything** I wanted to know was in that letter. I couldn't believe it. I said I wouldn't be mad right, but while I was reading this letter the devil said to me, "Now you know you can't just let him get away with this, even if you're not angry you have to at least act like it. I know you said you wouldn't be mad, but you can't just let this go like it's no big deal." The devil is really good at putting the wrong thoughts in your mind. I'm sure you've experienced it, that's a lesson for another chapter, but for now back to the story. That night when the phone call came, even though I wasn't angry, I acted as though I was. The conversation went something like this: Darren; "so did you get my letter?" Me; "yea, I got it" (because I was pretending to be mad, I wouldn't talk), Darren; "look, I knew when I wrote you this letter I was taking a chance on losing you and **I can't live my life without you!** But God has been dealing with me, and dealing with me, about confessing my sins to you and I said, 'God no way, why would I bring up something now that happened all those years ago, that she may never even know about. Why would I bring it up now and risk losing her?' But He said I *had* to, so I'm confessing my sins to you, I'm sorry and I'm asking that you would please forgive me for all the wrong I've ever done. I don't want to lose you and I promise you this day that I'll never lie to you again." I had no idea that God had been dealing with him all this time, but God did, that's probably why He put it on my heart to ask for the truth. The thing about God is while He's dealing with you on one end, he's always dealing with somebody else on the other to get you your answer. When I hung up the phone that night I fell on my face before God and began to cry tears of joy and thanked Him, because I knew at that point that I had received what I prayed for.

After that day I didn't have to ask anymore. I **knew** that he was a changed man. The Darren that I knew wasn't going to confess anything, even if you caught him in the very act, he would convince you that you didn't see what you know you just saw. I knew indeed that he was a different person and after that, I felt a trust that I hadn't felt before with him and I began to listen to him and follow him as he followed Christ and we became best friends **for real.** In other words, I began to respect him. How many of you know that RESPECT is the most important thing for a man? He can't lead you if you don't respect him, or should I say you won't follow. Men are funny when they don't feel respected. There are a lot of things that they don't do for you that they would otherwise if they felt that respect. All things considered, if a man is in his right mind, he will

do just about anything for you if you honor him
properly. Sometimes there may be other things
involved. He may need deliverance in some areas
of his life before you can minister to him
properly. For instance, if there are mental
challenges or something of that nature, things
that may cause him to act out of character. In
which case you may need to stay away because it
could cost you your life, for many women it has!

God shared this scripture with me after
going through this process. 1 Peter 3:6 AMP,

> *"It was thus that Sarah obeyed
> Abraham {following his guidance and
> acknowledging his headship over her
> by} calling him lord (master, leader,
> authority), And you are now her true
> daughters if you do right and let
> nothing terrify you {not giving way to
> hysterical fears or letting anxieties
> unnerve you}."*

The bottom line was, I needed to get out of fear
and in faith. I was afraid to let my guard down in
spite of the changes I was seeing because all of
the prior disappointments had fear deep rooted
on the inside of me. I also came to the conclusion

around that same time that I couldn't live for Darren. I wasn't responsible for how he lived his life. For years I worried about what other people would think if he hadn't really changed. You know that carrying the burden of what other people think can weigh you down for sure. But I decided that whatever he did or didn't do had no reflection on who I was or wasn't. I decided that I was going to love him freely and honor him just like it was in my heart to do and if he messed up and went back to prison, that would be on him not me. I finally stepped out of fear and into faith. Remember perfect love casteth out all fear. The fear was only there to torment me anyway. Once I let go of the fear then I wasn't worried about him going back to jail anymore. This was probably about 7 or 8 years before he even came home. That's how the enemy does you; he can have you so caught up with what could happen later that you can't even enjoy the **now.**

I didn't always listen to Darren. I'm not trying to come across to you like I was this perfect person because I was far from it, and will never be, but I am striving to get better every day! As I was saying I didn't always listen, and of course as you know, listening to him equates to the respect factor I was speaking of. Well one day, I was sitting in a church service on a Wednesday night, and I heard a voice down in my gut say, "start listening to your husband" and I responded, "Yes, I'm going to start listening to my husband." I thought I had been already, but what I realized is that it was always after it filtered through my thought process. In other words, I wouldn't just act on whatever he was saying because he said so. I had to determine rather I thought it was the right thing to do first. I'm not saying as women, you should just do whatever your husband says without thinking at all, that's not what I mean. But most of you can attest to the fact that he has asked you to do or not to do something that you didn't listen to because you felt that he didn't know what he was talking about at the time. Only to find out later that you should've listened. You'll know if you have the problem I had, because he'll tell you things like, "you don't listen to me" or "you don't respect me". If he ever says that to you then you probably don't listen to him and if you don't listen to him it may be because you don't feel like you can trust him. That was my problem, but as you can see all throughout this story God had to set up situations to help rebuild the trust that had been destroyed.

He told me once, "if there's a problem in our relationship, tell me and I'll fix it." I hung on to those words they rang in my heart. It made me feel like he was in control and I could trust him to make things right when I felt they were wrong. One day he called me crying, don't mistake his tears for weakness, he wasn't weak at all, but by this time he had become more sensitive to the Holy Spirit and wanted everything in his life to be right. When I heard his voice, I asked, "Daddy, what's wrong?" He said, "I just want to make sure that you're not an idol in my life, I love you so much, man I love you more than I love myself." My worried face changed to a smile. I said "Daddy, don't worry I'm not an idol. It's funny that you even said that." I said "God gave me your answer just the other day and I had no idea that you were even thinking this. I was driving down the street the other day talking to God and I said, 'Lord we love each other so much and I know there is no way that we could have the kind of love that we have for each other with all that we've gone through, except that you put it in us'." And God said back to me, "You keep loving each other the way you do because you loving him the way you do is your way of loving Me and him loving you the way he does is him loving Me. You see, I'm not there in the flesh for you to show physical love to, so when you love each other that way that's your expression of love to Me." I said, "'WOW' Lord, okay that's what you were talking about when you said the marriage relationship is supposed to represent the relationship between Christ and His church." I said, "so you see Daddy, I'm not an idol at all, you just keep right on loving me the way you do, it's how God wants us."

There was also a time that he called me and told me about something that was going on with our daughter. My first thought was, "how did you know that?" So I asked him, who told him that, because there was no way he could've known that without me telling him. He said to me "Baby, I know my kids, I know **all** of them. You think just because I'm not there, that I don't know my kids. I told you, I pray for you all everyday and God gives me the wisdom to lead my family. He tells me what's going on with my children so that I know what to tell you to do." I was convinced at that point that he was really connected to us and that he had to be praying for us in order to know the things that he had been sharing with me. There were many times like these when he said things to me that were monumental moments for me, because they were trust builders. You can imagine that there wasn't much trust in our relationship before, at least not when it came to protection and direction. I was never concerned about other women though, I knew he loved me the only way he *could*, I just needed him to be free so that he could love me the way he *should*.

Chapter 5

The Season of Waiting: Change God's Way

HOW I SAW US FREE

If I said it once, I must've said it a thousand times, "Lord I thank you that Darren loves you with all of his heart, soul, mind and strength and loves me as Christ loves the church and gave Himself for it." Romans 4:17 says that God is a God that gives life to the dead and calls those things which be not as though they were. You have to constantly speak the Word of God over your situation, but you have to know the Word in order to speak it. I'm amazed at how many people say that they LOVE God, they're LIVING for God and even say that they KNOW God, yet have no idea of who God is. They have no idea of the love of God that goes deeper than the ocean. God says in John 3:16 that he sent his only son to die for you. Can you imagine what that really means? Think about your child or children if you have any. Do you have one that you would be willing to give up for everyone else to go free, especially for people who aren't even thinking about you, people who are doing their own thing, twisting what you said to satisfy their own evil desires. Those same people that he was being sacrificed for are the very ones that mistreated, abused and eventually murdered him. He paid such an awesome price for you and it shouldn't be taken for granted. If you really understood how much God has already provided for you, you wouldn't be wasting your time and energy pursuing things that don't matter, you would be pursuing Him. You need to **know** Him like you need your next breath. That's why God tells us in 2 Timothy 2:15 to study to show ourselves approved unto God a workman that needeth not to be ashamed, rightly dividing the word of truth.

I've been told several times by young people of this generation that *"people don't wait anymore." "They run at the first sign of trouble." "Nobody is praying through anymore." "There aren't any people left like your generation."* Now, certainly I wouldn't advise anyone to knowingly go get in a relationship where your spouse would have all of these issues going on, but the skills I used will work for any kind of issue in relationships. Don't judge but love! Love people into change. Above all else love each other because love covers over a multitude of sin. (1 Peter 4:8) Most marital problems come from us being selfish, try being selfless instead. Treat your husband like he's already doing everything right. He already knows he doesn't deserve it, so it will cause him to change his ways. God said that it was his goodness that drew men unto repentance, not our nagging.

I spent many nights praying and allowing God to speak to me. It's funny because most of the revelation came with God bringing correction to me. I remember before Darren went to prison, I told God, "all we need is for Darren to stop doing drugs and we'll be alright. We don't have any more issues." God said, "oh yea, let's talk about Tonya." I said, "WHAT!" He said, "Let's look at you." I said "ah man." When God got through showing me all the areas in my life that needed to change I said, "Ooh Lord I thought I had a right to leave him, I need to be thanking you that he didn't leave me." I was violent; I'm telling you I would swing on him in a minute because I didn't know any other way to get back at him for what he was doing to me. I wanted him to pay for the pain he was causing! I would swing on him as he walked through the door, I would be so angry. God had to deliver me from that and from the pain as well.

During this time I learned how to develop my relationship with God. I began a journey of my own. Darren was on a journey in prison, but I had my own journey to take. I remember sitting on my bed reading the book of Proverbs. I had read a couple of times about this "nagging wife." Proverbs 21:9 says,

> *"It is better to live in a corner on the roof than inside the house with a quarreling wife."*

Proverbs 21:19 says

> *"It's better to live alone in the desert than with a quarreling and complaining wife".*

So I kept on reading, and after a while there it was again. Proverbs 25:24 says,

> "It's better to live in a corner on the roof than inside the house with a quarreling wife."

Then there it was again! Proverbs 27:15 says

> "A quarreling wife is as bothersome as a continual dripping on a rainy day. Stopping her is like stopping the wind."

I said "Man, Lord you act like this woman is hard to live with." He said **"SHE IS."** When He said **SHE IS**, I felt it deep inside my core. I repented that night and promised God that I would never nag him again. Darren had told me many times before that I was nagging him, but of course I wasn't listening. I thought he just didn't want to hear the truth. I began to understand how difficult it was for men to handle our mouths. They're not equipped to handle us going on and on about something, it makes their head hurt. That's why they'll leave the house or tell you to be quiet. It may appear that they are being mean or insensitive, but in reality they're just not made up that way.

There are ways to get what you want from your husband. If you'll treat him right, he'll give you the world. First off, RESPECT him! Without the respect, the other things aren't as important. When a man feels disrespected in his own home, it opens the door for him to do things he shouldn't: like have affairs, stay out all night, or treat you in a disrespectful manner. It also keeps him from doing the things that he should, like showering you with love, attention and GIFTS, yes lots of GIFTS. It's also important to give him what he wants sexually (I'm talking to married women, not the singles). A satisfied man is a happy man and a happy man will give you whatever you want. If you pay attention in a relationship you begin to notice what kinds of things please the other person and you can began to do those without being asked. Then there are times when you don't know their preference but ask them so that you don't assume the wrong thing. If you're single stop selling yourself cheap. Don't give away your goods for free. Let him marry you first and if you think he won't wait, well he may not, but the **right** one will. If you think you need to sleep with him to keep him, you're deceived already, because nine times out of ten he's not going to marry you anyway. He'll use you for as long as you let him. Then when the right one comes along who demands respect, he'll leave you and marry her quickly because that's what he's been looking for and he doesn't want to lose her. You'll find that you gave him all of you for no reason at all. Man after man, will take from you with absolutely no intent to stay with you.

You see, men can be content without getting married for a long time, and if you're giving him everything that you would give him if you were married, then what does he need to marry you for? In his mind, it's easier for him to walk away if he doesn't marry you, so he'll sleep with you, live with you, even have kids with you with no intent to marry you. You'll just be all used up and he'll go and marry someone else and think nothing of it. Men tend to use women as what I like to call, "time fillers." Meaning, they'll stay with you telling you anything you want to hear to keep you around and to keep from being alone. But it's only until they find MRS. Right. You're not it, but because they don't like being alone and they still want their needs to be met, they'll string you along for however long it takes for them to come across the right one or until **you** get tired of being the "time filler." You have to be smart enough to be in control of the relationship yourself. What I mean by that is, never allow yourself to be used in the first place. Besides, you don't want there to be a long list of men who have the privilege of saying "I've been with her," because it is a privilege. Love yourself enough to say, **I'M WORTH THE WAIT!** Stop telling yourself that, "you have needs too." You do have them but you can wait until *Mr. Right* shows up to get them fulfilled, stop thinking that you can't.

I've heard plenty of adults advising young people to date for long periods of time before getting married or live together and get to know each other first. I've even heard them say that there's nothing wrong with one-night stands. All of that may feel good to your flesh, but it's not the will of God for you to behave in that manner. Once you gain understanding of how unclean sex outside of marriage is in the sight of God, you'll stop. Romans 12:1-2 in the Message Bible says,

> *"So here's what I want you to do, God helping you: Take your everyday, ordinary life—your sleeping, eating, going-to-work, and walking-around life—and place it before God as an offering. Embracing what God does for*

you is the best thing you can do for him. Don't become so well adjusted to your culture that you fit into it without even thinking. Instead, fix your attention on God. You'll be changed from the inside out. Readily recognize what he wants from you, and quickly respond to it. Unlike the culture around you, always dragging you down to its level of immaturity, God brings the best out of you, develops well-formed maturity in you."

The King James Version says in Romans 12:1,

"I beseech you therefore, brethren, by the mercies of God, that ye present your bodies a living sacrifice, holy, acceptable unto God, which is your reasonable service."

In other words it's the least you can do.

Realize that you don't have to compromise yourself in order to get a good man, and there are still some good men out there. All you need is one. 1Corinthians 6:18-20 says,

"Run away from sexual sin. Every other sin people do is outside their bodies, but those who sin sexually sin against their own bodies. 19You should know that your body is a temple for the Holy Spirit who is in you. You have received the Holy Spirit from God. So, you do not belong to yourselves 20 because you were bought by God for a price. So honor God with your bodies."

Besides, you don't just get married to "say" you have a husband. When God puts two people together it's for a divine purpose. There's something He wants the two of you to accomplish. You will fit each other. If you're on one accord, walking together in the same direction, fulfilling God's divine purpose for your union, then marriage can be blissful and the most beautiful relationship on the face of the earth. Not many people experience it that way though, only because they haven't learned to put their mate before themselves. When you do that, it eliminates those feelings of being used and unappreciated. So single ladies, marry Jesus until Mr. Right finds you.

I know you're probably thinking that people don't discipline themselves that way anymore, not only are women sleeping with men before marriage, but women are sleeping with women and men with men. It seems as if there's no standard at all for keeping yourself out of fornication and adultery. God's principles seem to have been thrown out completely, but God hasn't changed. The world has but God hasn't, and He rewards faithfulness. That's Who my commitment was to. I loved Darren Brown, but I loved God more and that's what kept me all those years. Plus Darren worshipped the ground I walked on. I told him I'd rather have him locked up, than most of the men who were free. I don't know what I did to deserve such a wonderful gift. Well actually every woman in the world deserves to have a man that loves her with all of his heart; once you've experienced that kind of love, you'll realize that there is no other way to have it.

Let me clarify something, God wasn't always first in my life. I thought He was, but He wasn't. You'll recall earlier that I mentioned being spiritually slapped in the face. Over the course of my life I've been slapped more than a few times, but this occasion that I'm about to share was actually the first time. Darren had been gone maybe a year or two, I don't remember exactly, but as I was praying to God crying my heart out "Please give him back, I'll do anything, I'll cook, I'll clean, I'll do whatever I need to do." He did all or most of the cooking and most of the cleaning along with taking care of the kids. He ironed my uniforms for work a lot of times, and even bathed me at night when I got home. He would literally have my bath water ready and waiting and physically bathed me and put me in the bed. During this time I was managing a restaurant and would get home late, most nights 12:30am, but as late as two or three on the weekends. At any rate, I was crying my heart out and I thought that if I started doing some of the things that the woman usually does like cooking and cleaning, that God would give him back to me. But to my surprise, as I was balling my eyes out, what I got was a slap in the face. The Holy Spirit said to me, "That's what got you in this mess in the first place. You loved him more than you did Me." I said, "OUCH!" I immediately began drying up my tears and as I was wiping my face, I said to the Lord holding my hands up as if He were standing in front of me, "Hold that thought, hold that thought Lord, let me go and search my heart, cause I dare not lie to the Holy Spirit." I walked away and about 2 days later I came back to that exact spot of prayer and said "Lord you were right, I didn't know when you were asking me to keep myself and I thought I couldn't do it, that I was placing him before You. I didn't realize that I was making him "my god" and for that I am **eternally** sorry. I can tell You this day though, "I love you more." I said, "you are the only person who can say 'I'll never leave nor forsake you' and mean it." I said, "he wants to be here now, but he's not. You're the only one who can make that promise and back it up, so I say to You that I do indeed love You more. I'll never make the mistake of placing him or anything else before You again." I used to say that I couldn't live without Darren Brown, but I came to the realization that, JESUS was the only person that I couldn't live without.

This was another very valuable lesson that I learned. You see, with women most of us will compromise our standards a little or sometimes a lot for a man we think we love. I had been compromising for years. That's why I'm begging you not to. I can tell you that it's not worth it. The pleasure you get out of sin is not worth the price you have to pay for it. You see, the price tag for sin isn't like the price tag at the mall. When you want something you look at the tag and see how much it costs, then you can determine whether you want to pay for it or not. With sin you don't know the price until you're paying for it. "You can choose the sin, but you can't choose the consequence," I heard somebody say once.

Darren and I spent a lot of time believing that he would somehow get out of prison early and we wouldn't have to do all of this time. After a while though, we realized that we were going to have pay for our decisions and 15 years was the price tag. Nobody could pray us out, if this is what I had to endure to pay for what I had done then so be it, at least I didn't have to go to hell for it. You see, God is a good Father and He's not trying to keep anything good from us. He's only trying to protect us and keep us from going through so much unnecessary heartache and pain by telling us what to do and what not to do. Remember He only wants to bless you and not harm you in any way. Look at the relationship you're in right now. Are you married? And then are you married to the opposite sex? Now let me ask you, did you do it God's way? And by God's way I mean, did you ask

God to lead you or tell you if this was the right man before you said yes. Did you refrain from having sex until you were married? What about taking him to meet your parents or even your Pastor for their approval before getting involved? Doing things like this will help keep you safe. Sometimes other people can see things in a person that you may not be able see. They're not blinded by love like you are at the moment.

If you didn't seek wise counsel before getting into your relationship and you're feeling frustrated or overwhelmed with your current situation, the first thing I want you to do is STOP! Repent for not asking God first and then allow Him to turn your mistake into a victorious situation however He wants to do that. It's never too late to turn things around, so don't beat yourself up another minute. Just ask God what you need to do next to fix this and He's faithful to lead you every step of the way. Whoever you're with right now may not be the right person for you, so your answer may be to sever that relationship. On the other hand, it's a possibility that you're with your soul mate and you're just facing some challenges that you're not sure how to handle. Praying and asking God how to help him may be your answer. You may be trying to help but it may not be the help he needs. Sometimes men will tell us how to help them but because we're not in the habit of really listening to them we don't hear it. There were times when I would spend hours in prayer asking God what to do about certain situations and he would tell me to get up and do what Darren had already told me to do about the situation. Sometimes, he would say, "listen to Darren, he's telling you what's wrong, you don't have to ask me." I realized that we often put ourselves through a lot of unnecessary grief. If we would just apologize when we are wrong, or ask questions like, "what is it that I can do to fix this?" we could save ourselves valuable time and energy that can be spent building up our relationships opposed to tearing them down. A soft answer turns away wrath and sometimes that's all you need to have peace and the love of God in your home. I know as women, we feel that we are right most of the time and you may very well be, but understanding the way your husband thinks can be tricky, so even when you believe you're right, hear him out. It may be that both of you are right you just needed some understanding.

Men are ego driven, so spend more time complimenting your husband and building up his ego rather than complaining about the characteristics you don't like. You will be amazed at how far this will take you. The more you build him up and cover him with prayer, the more he changes into the man that you want him to be. And please, please, please stop comparing him with other men. Your husband has gifts and talents in him that are unique to him and are to be cherished. He can only be who God called him to be, nobody else. If you spend time appreciating who God gave you, then you'll spend less time comparing him to somebody else. Besides that's not fair to him, and I'm sure you don't want him comparing you to other women.

When your husband shares his vision with you, don't knock it down, nurture it and protect it. You do that by praying for him, seeking God for wisdom, building him up not tearing him down. Proverbs 14:1 says,

*"A **wise** woman builds her house but a foolish one tears hers down with her own hands."*

Proverbs 12:4 says,

"A good wife is like a crown for her husband, but a disgraceful wife is like a disease in his bones."

Proverbs 15:4 says,

"As a tree gives fruit, healing words give life."

In spite of what other people saw I saw him free and us back together prosperous and successful.

Some of you reading this book will decide TODAY that this is it for you. A light bulb has gone off in your head and you've been set free. You're ending that relationship right now and have made up your mind to wait on God's best for you. But others of you are hearing me and are not ready to make a change yet. You're still waddling in the deception of "maybe" or "what if." "What if he is the one for me or what if nobody else comes along, and I end up all alone?" "Maybe he'll change or maybe he'll marry me." I'm confident though, that you'll wake up and stop allowing yourself to be used. If you have to, keep reading this book over and over again. Go to the scripture references that I gave you and study them until you have enough faith to walk away.

Chapter 5 The Season of Waiting ; Change God's Way

Do me a favor. Don't waste your time and energy sitting around waiting on somebody to figure out what a great gift you are. If they don't recognize the value in you, keep it moving. If you form habits of being moved by someone else's perception of your value, your opinion of yourself may start to change and **you** even stop seeing the value in you. Remember you have to know you're a queen even if nobody else recognizes it. Don't allow someone else's opinion of you be the frame for how you see yourself.

I remember my Pastor saying years ago, "Most men's problems are silly women." They can only do to you what you allow them to, and if you're allowing it then you can't complain about it. A friend of mine once told me, "When you get sick and tired of being sick and tired of the devil, you'll stop putting up with him." I thought I was already sick and tired, but what I realized was when I **really** got sick and tired of him, I put him out just like she said. I said, "Devil that 'stupid' sign I had written across my forehead has been removed, I'm not stupid anymore!" Now, that can represent anything in your life that's not God for you, rather it be a person, situation or thing. All you have to do, without giving consideration to the circumstances or people around you is say, "Lord I only want what you want for me, EVERYTHING else has to go." The reason I said do it without consideration of anything else is because often times we'll hear God speak to us, but we rationalize it away or allow people to talk us out of it. The best way to end an ungodly or unhealthy relationship is to just walk away and don't look back. Trying to go back and explain often gets you entangled again, so just walk away. Stop allowing yourself to be manipulated in order to satisfy someone else's lust. Now if you have children by this person and you have to see him because of the children and you keep getting entangled that way, maybe you should have a mutual person involved. Somebody that he can pick the kids up from and drop them off to (a relative or close friend) until you are strong enough to see him and not melt.

Some of you may have ended a relationship with someone because you knew that he wasn't good for you but you still occasionally sleep with him in order to keep him around. Maybe you have a baby by this person and you feel that you need his child support to have enough every month. You allow him to run by your house whenever he feels like it, when you know that he's running by someone else's house as well. You're a wife, not somebody's woman on the side. You have to make him respect you as such; but first, **you** have to respect you as such. Women you hold the keys to your destiny, no one else. YOU CAN HAVE IT YOUR WAY! All you have to do is set the standard. The more you walk away and go back, the stronger the hold becomes and it gets harder and harder to get free.

I read this scripture one day and noticed something that I hadn't noticed before. Matthew 10:37 says,

> *"Those who love their son or daughter more than they love me are not worthy to be my followers."*

When I read that, I thought about the situations that I just spoke to you about. We're sleeping with the father of our children in order to keep him in their life, when we know that God is telling us not to. We're scared that he won't come around if we're not giving him something to come for. We fear that he won't buy diapers, formula and the countless other things that our children need. These are some of the things that cause us to put our son or daughter before the Lord, like I was doing. Only in my case it was Darren, not my kids. Isaiah 6:1 says,

"In the year that King Uzziah died, I saw the Lord sitting on a very high throne, "

I looked at that scripture and see me. When Darren was moved out of the way, I saw the Lord. Sometimes God has to allow people to be moved out of the way so that we can see him. As I shared with you earlier, I got Darren back, but it's definitely in perspective now.

Also, during this time of waiting, I spent a lot of days and nights crying. I never cried around the kids, but whenever I went to see Darren by myself, I would always cry walking back to the car. How do you keep your eyes on Jesus when they're full of tears? The hurt I felt at times would be over whelming. I told you it was a day-by-day process, sometimes even hour-by-hour or minute-by-minute. I would try to figure out how I could even make it through the night it would be so hard at times. Then I would go to bed that night, wishing he was there to hold me, sometimes imagining him making love to me, well a lot of times imagining him making love to me, fall asleep, wake up in the morning and realize that I had made it through another night. Having that spiritual and emotional support was great, not just great but necessary, although I did miss the physical bonding. It's hard when you're in love with a person you can hardly touch. I considered it to be one of those, "so close yet so far" kind of things.

We also spent a lot of money on the phone bill, because talking to him in bed until I fell asleep also helped me to make it to the next day. That's literally how I made it through those initial 12 ½ years. The funny thing about it was that he felt the same way. He said that he would be balled up in his bed, heartbroken after every visit. Even though he waited very excitedly for every visit, he also hated them because of the way he would feel afterwards. When we left he wanted to leave with us but couldn't, so the visits were very hard on him. He said they drained him. He could always tell when somebody had just come from a visit because they always went to lie down.

One thing is for sure, only being able to express your love verbally improved our communication skills. We learned how to talk about **everything** and we also learned how to really listen to each other, even though we didn't like the circumstances under which we were learning. I know as a woman that communication is vitally important in any relationship, but especially in a marriage. You don't want your husband in the deepest parts of you at night but rarely has anything to say to you in the day. It makes you feel used and mistreated. So, attaining those communication skills were very valuable to our relationship. Good communication can serve as foreplay for a woman. Every woman wants a man who listens to and understands her. Men are built to solve problems, so you know if he really listens to you then he'll solve whatever problem you're having if you think something is wrong. When he solves problems, you feel protected and that creates a bond, which in turn creates intimacy and a great desire for making love.

For most women whose husbands or boyfriends are in prison, **if** they're waiting at all, it's usually not for a long period of time, which is understandable. Maybe six months to two years and even then she may not be faithful. She may still be going to visit him and talking to him on the phone and even putting money on his books, because she does care about him, but sleeping with someone else all the while. She's not going to put her love life on hold for him. She may or may not be able to hook up with him once he's home, but she doesn't want to be alone in the meantime. There are a lot of lonely nights in waiting. The only reason I didn't consider being with someone else was because sexual sin was what got me into this situation in the first place. On top of that I loved God too much by now to intentionally disappoint Him. So I never even thought about being with someone else. Besides I wanted intimacy and love making, not sex, and he was the only person that I had ever loved.

I remember once when Darren was sent to another state. It was too far for me to drive all the time like I had been doing before, so I had to fly. When he first arrived there, I flew down every month to see him, but by the fifth or sixth month I couldn't get a flight two months in a row. A friend of mine called me and said that she had a dream that Darren was wrapped up like a mummy and really needed to see me. She said, "he's not doing well he really can't take not seeing you, so if I have to go with you to help you drive, I will, but you have to go." It was at that point that I realized that we were being sustained by each other's love. He really couldn't make it without seeing me. His being able to see and touch me was what enabled him to function in there. It's literally what kept him from being institutionalized, which simply means being in prison for so long that you no longer know how to function in the outside world.

WHY I WAITED

People often ask me now that it's over, why I waited or sometimes they'll tell me that there's no way they could have or would have waited. My own husband didn't understand how or why I waited. He didn't even believe that I would wait. He thought, "She's young and beautiful, she could have anybody she wants. She's not going to waste her time waiting on me." Besides that, he didn't think that it was fair for me to put my life on hold for him that way. He wanted me to, he just didn't think that I would. On top of the fact, that the men in prison were telling him that there was no way that I would wait, and he was crazy if he thought that I would and certainly not faithfully even if I did wait. That's why he wanted me to leave him early into his sentence. He figured me leaving was inevitable so the sooner the better, then he could quit worrying about when I was going to drop this bombshell on him.

He had seen many guys receive "Dear John" letters since he arrived, as well as inmates tearing the phone off of the wall because their wife or girlfriend had just informed them that they couldn't wait on them any longer. But the fact that he'd tell me things like, "Nobody else in the world could love me better than he could and that our ending would be far greater than our beginning" and the many times that he would call me with a word straight from the Lord, all convinced me to stay. Darren hearing from God meant more to me than anything else. That's all I ever wanted in the first place. I also remembered the fact that God had promised me that what he was going to do in Darren's life later, would be an undeniable miracle in comparison to what his life was like then. My faith was committed to seeing what the end was going to be. Even if I had turned my back on Darren I couldn't turn my back on God, so I made up in my mind that I would wait as long as it took, which is exactly what I did. After he realized that I wasn't going to leave, he then began to relax. He says it actually took him a lot longer than he let on, somewhere around eight or nine years. I thought that it happened much earlier.

Several people told me that I must have been crazy during this journey, because just like him, they thought that I was young and beautiful and should go on with my life. My own mother even told me that maybe I should start dating other people, but I never had any desire to do that. I guess though, I wasn't really thinking about what other people were thinking. I was only doing what was in my heart to do. Besides, most of the married couples that I saw weren't happy, so I didn't see how leaving him, because he was in prison, for somebody that was out here would be any more beneficial for me. I just figured that I could be most happy with somebody that loved me more than life, no matter where he was, than to take my chances on somebody who loved himself more than he could love me.

Besides all of that, when you have history with a person, usually you don't want to give that up and start over. I mean I had been with Darren since I was 15 years old. I had spent all of my adult years thus far with him, and we had children together. I wanted my children to be raised by their own father, not some other man. And besides the drug scene, I loved everything else about him. At this point in our lives, he was becoming my dream husband. This wasn't the time for me to leave, so somebody else who hadn't put in any work, could come along and be blessed by this awesome man of God that I had carried along in prayer for so long. She would have been reaping where she hadn't planted and I wasn't having that!

Chapter 6

How God Blessed & Provided For Us

One day while I was praying, I was asking God to bless Darren to be able to bless me when he came home, because I knew how badly in his heart he wanted to do for me. While I was asking God this, out of my mouth in a prophetic voice came "I will repay saith the Lord all that the cankerworm has taken." Before I could finish the prophecy I stopped and started screaming (because I was new in the Word at the time and very excited) "hey that's in the Word," I exclaimed. So I ran to get my Bible and looked it up, it's in Joel 2:25. God was telling me that day that He would pay us back for all of the trouble. I didn't know how at the time but He did.

I was managing a restaurant when Darren went to prison. I remember on several different occasions standing in the lobby of that restaurant all alone with my hands lifted towards heaven, asking God what He wanted me to do with my life. I would say, "God I know this can't be my fate in life, what am I supposed to be doing?" One time He told me to just keep learning how to run the business so that I could run my own business one day. I had no idea what kind of business He was talking about, so I said, "what business?" But He didn't tell me at the time.

When my youngest daughter was born I had taken her to a family friend who had a home daycare. She had kept my oldest two for about a year when they were born then Darren and I kept them ourselves. I worked evenings at least three of the five workdays, so he kept them while I was at work. At any rate, I took my youngest daughter to her because Darren was already gone by the time she was born. After six months she told my Mom that she wasn't keeping infants during the summer so I needed to find someone else to keep her. For a whole year I took her to different places and it was always some reason why I had to move her. Eventually, I would have to leave her with my mother or my sister while I was seeking out the right care. My mom worked so she couldn't keep her all the time during the day. She always kept her in the evenings though.

One day I wasn't sure who was going to keep her and I ended up taking her to my sister's. On my way to work that day I was furious. I'm the kind of person that likes stability for my children, so I hated the feeling of not knowing where she'd be from day to day. I said, "God you said if I ask, I would receive; if I seek, I would find and if I knocked the door would be opened unto me (Matthew 6:7). Well I've been asking, I've been seeking and I've been knocking; NOW YOU HAVE TO ANSWER ME! If you don't tell me something that I can do to come home and take care of my own baby, I'm going to quit this job. Now I don't know how we're going to eat, but I'm coming off of this job today because I'm not going to be passing my baby all around like that." It's funny how when you get serious with God, He gets serious with you. He said to me very clearly, "do what I told you to do 4 years ago." I said, "WHAT?! You mean I'm supposed to be doing daycare." He said, "Yes and do it right so that I can bless it!" Four years ago I had quit my job and was going to do daycare in my home, but I didn't have a clue what I was doing. I ended up getting on food stamps and even got behind on my mortgage for the first time. That's what happens when you have zeal without knowledge (Proverbs 19:2), so after about 9 months I went back to work. I didn't know then that God was telling me to do the daycare, I thought it was just something I had thought about doing. But when He said to me, "Do what I told you to do four years ago," I knew exactly what He was talking about. When I got to work I immediately called to our state-licensing unit and inquired about what I needed to do to start this daycare. I worked very diligently at getting it done. I had heard the Lord's voice so clearly, I had never heard anything so clearly before in my life. I was super excited because I knew it would work. It's funny because I didn't have any fear. I've never been as bold and confident as I was when I took on this venture.

All of my family thought I was crazy to quit my job. Darren was hesitant because this time God spoke it to me and not him initially. So he wasn't sure that I should be quitting my job either (God did confirm that for him later). He said, "I don't mind you doing it, just wait until I get home so if it doesn't work I can have your back." I said, "I understand how you feel Daddy, but you don't have to have my back, God's got me this time."

I started out simple because I didn't have a lot of extra money to invest. I bought the least expensive things on the list of things that they told me I had to purchase. As I built my clientele, I purchased more things and eventually I had a full supply. I loved and nurtured those children and educated them and tried to provide the most fun environment that I could. We did lots of math, science, reading and art. They learned the different types of music and we cooked in the classroom at least once a week. I loved to see children happy, so I was always taking them on field trips and finding exciting things for them to do. They didn't want to go home in the evenings and couldn't wait to come back in the mornings. God had told me to do it right so that He could bless it and that's what I did. God did bless it and we lived a good life while Darren was gone. We weren't rich but we were far better off than we were when I was managing that restaurant.

I recall one day, I was riding down the street praying, this was before I opened the daycare, and I asked God to bless my business. His response to me was, "Meditate on this book of the law that thou mayest observe to do according to all that is written therein, then YOU shall make your OWN way prosperous Tonya and then YOU shall have good success." I said, "Okay Lord, that's Joshua 1:8." When you meditate on the word of God, it's easy for God to lead you by his Spirit and because He knows everything, He can tell you what to do, how to do it, what to purchase and what will be a waste of your time and money. Anything you want to know, He has the answer. Once I began to seek Him, and follow his instructions, then I could do things right and He could bless it, just like He said.

One day while still working at the restaurant, I decided to ride through this subdivision. Now I couldn't afford a new home at the time, but I wanted to dream, so I went through every block in this subdivision writing down all of the addresses that were for sale, along with the listing agent and phone number. When I got to the end of the subdivision I start calling numbers for prices. I was so discouraged when I got done that I just sat there and cried my eyes out.

I said, "Lord, this is the kind of life that I want for my children but I don't know any way that I can get it. I didn't go to school to be a doctor or lawyer and I'm not faulting You for that, I'm just saying I didn't prepare myself for that" because at that time those were the only people I knew that lived that kind of life. I said, "I don't have any rich relatives to leave me any inheritance or anything like that, at least not that I know of, but You told me that if I delighted myself in You, that You would give me the desires of my heart and I am so delighted in serving You. I don't have anything else, so if You don't do it for me it can't be done." I left that subdivision that day feeling sick and hopeless.

I had never been hopeless before, but that's what I felt that day. I just didn't see any way out of my current state. As I was riding down the street I saw a sign on this building that said something about cell phones, so I turned and went inside. Now I had been trying to get a cell phone for several months and everywhere I went they wanted me to pay a large deposit. Anywhere from $250-750 and I'm thinking to myself, "I know this can't be right, because I know some people who have one and I know they didn't spend that kind of money because they didn't have that kind of money." So I just kept refusing and looking for a better offer. Well when I went inside this particular company they were having a special sale with zero deposit and they even gave me the phone for free. It was like God was wrapping His arms around me that day saying, "don't give up just hold on, we're going somewhere." To somebody else that may not have meant anything, but knowing what I knew, I knew that God was talking to me and I was encouraged to keep going until the day would come when I **could** afford one of those houses and a better life for my children.

I stayed faithful at the restaurant. Even though I didn't want to be there I operated with a spirit of excellence. After all, they were paying me to do a job so I always gave 100%, until God called me off of that job and began to bless me beyond my expectations. Right in the middle of my spanking, (for not keeping myself when God asked me to) God began to raise me up. Our children lived a blessed life, lacking nothing and we were able to help a lot of people over the years.

I remember several years ago going to the Infinity and Lexus dealerships. I wasn't going to buy anything I just wanted to look. Before he left

Darren and I would casually talk about which cars we liked with no intention of buying. We would see different ones riding by sometimes and would comment on which one we preferred. Well one day I decided to go to the dealership to see how much one of the luxury cars cost. I couldn't afford one, I was just curious to know. This was probably 18 or 19 years ago. I asked the salesman how much they were and he responded $40-$50,000. I'm thinking to myself, "Lord, how can anybody afford to pay that much for a car?" At the time we were buying $10,000 cars and that was a struggle. I said, "What do they do? Do they pay $1000/month for like 10 years or something or do they have rich parents to buy it for them." I just couldn't fathom how people could afford this, but I said to the salesman, **"I'll be back"**. I didn't know how or when, but I believed God that some kind of way I would be back to get one.

Fast forward several years, I'm riding down the street and I see a Lexus ride by. I started laughing and said "God's going to give me one of those, watch and see. I'm not going to stress over it or try to figure it out how but watch and see won't he give me one." So for the next couple of months, every time I saw one I would say that.

One day I was at the dentist office and an ad for the Lexus dealership came on the radio and I felt impressed in my spirit that I was supposed to go buy one. I said, "Oh no Lord, I'm not buying a car today, I already have one car payment, I'm not about to have two." But the feeling wouldn't go away, so I thought, "well I do have somewhere to go that's near the dealership, so I'll stop by there but I'm not buying anything."

As I was headed to the Lexus dealership I said, "I don't even have any of my papers with me so I know I'm not buying anything." Being self-employed, I had to show my life's history every time I wanted to purchase something and I didn't have any of that paperwork with me so I knew I couldn't purchase a new car even if I had wanted to.

I headed over to the dealership anyway and when I got there, we went through their process and to make a long story short I found a car that I liked and took it for a test-drive. I asked the lady that was helping me something about being self-employed, I'm not sure what exactly, but whatever I asked her, her assumption was that I wasn't going to buy this car. (You know how people act when they think you can't afford something.) Well when we got back to the dealership, she went inside and I was still in the parking lot. So I say to God, "Look, you don't just get up in the morning and go buy a car. You talk about it, you plan for it, you don't just get up one morning and go buy one."

When I look back now, I realize that God was trying to change the way I thought, from poverty to wealth, and as you can see I was fighting every step of the way, unintentionally of course.

I thought to myself, "I haven't even talked to my husband today; we haven't even talked about buying a car." Before I could even finish my thought, my phone rang. I said, "I can't believe this Daddy, guess what? I'm at the Lexus dealership and the Holy Spirit is telling me to buy this car. I just told him that I hadn't talked to you today and you call, so what do you want me to do?" He said, "If they can do this, this, and this buy it, if they can't, don't." I said, "Okay." Let me just say, that that was the easiest thing I have ever purchased.

I know some people struggle with people purchasing cars on credit and say that couldn't have been God, but I can only relay to you what happened, the way it happened. God would eventually elevate us to a place that we could purchase cars without credit.

Ten months later, Darren tells me to take the car back and purchase a truck. I said, "Daddy I can't do that. I haven't even had that car a year yet, you can't just be buying cars and taking them back like that, I don't even have any equity built up in it yet." He said, "Yes you can! The same way they gave you that one they're going to give you this one. Take it back! I want you to drive a SUV they're safer." I said, "Well which truck am I supposed to buy? "He said, "You'll know when you get there." I said, "Okay." I go to the dealership again. I say, "I don't know what I'm supposed to be buying I'm only here at my husband's request. He told me to buy a truck, now I don't know what truck, but I'm supposed to buy a truck."

So the salesman took me outside to look at the trucks. We found one that I liked and took it for a test-drive. I said, "I like the truck but you don't have a color that I want." He said, "Ah come on Mrs. Brown you're not going to buy the truck because of the color?" I said, "No! Why would I buy a car and it not be what I wanted. I don't care if I get this truck or not, it makes me no difference, like I said, I'm only here at my husband's request!"

At that moment, somebody rides onto the lot in another truck and he says to me, "Mrs. Brown, here comes one now, do you like the color of that one? I said, "As a matter of fact I do." He said, "Well I'm going to put a sold sign on it." I said, "You can't do that, whoever's driving it may want it." He said, "Yes I can," and he did, so we went inside to do the paperwork. While we were sitting there, I said to him, "let me go and look at the truck, I don't even know what it looks like on the inside." As I was looking at it, I said to myself, "I don't think I even like this one, because I don't know what all of this stuff is inside. It had all of this stuff in the roof." Just as I was getting out on one side to go and tell him that I didn't want it, he was opening the door on the other side. I hadn't seen him come out. He says so excitedly, "Mrs. Brown you got a T.V." I said "oh, is that what that is? I was just about to tell you that I didn't want it, because I didn't know what all of that stuff was."

Now they put the T.V.'s on the headrest but back then they were in the roof and you had to open them up, so I didn't know what it was. Anyway, I said, "well if I buy one it has to be this one because my baby has been asking me for a T.V. for the past several months and apparently God wants to give her one. I told her the next time I bought a car that I would get one with a T.V. in it." I was talking about the next van for the kids, not my car and we had recently bought a new van already, so a T.V. wasn't even on my mind. I said, "Lord you mean this baby is six years old and you're giving her the desires of her heart. I don't want a T.V. she does and you're giving it to her."

God was showing me that He didn't just care about my desires, but He cared about my children's desires as well. I said, "Lord, you're some kind of God!"

After I got home that evening, I was on the phone with my friend and she asked me if I was going to buy the car. I had driven it home but I was supposed to go back on Monday to finish the paperwork. I said, "I don't know, I don't want to be spending all of my money on houses and cars. As I was saying that, I was walking into my living room and could see the truck in my driveway. At that moment, I heard a voice say, "I'm trying to take you to another level and you're contemplating whether or not you want to go." I said to my friend, "Oh yea, I'm buying it, I just made up my mind (she didn't hear what I heard).

God said to me, "This is not about you. I'm doing this for My glory. I want single sisters to know that if they'll trust me I'll do it for them." He said, "They're selling their souls for $30." Much more than that today, cause a good weave will run $200 or more, but this was 2001. He said, "$30 to get their hair done, $30 to get their nails done, they need $30 for gas or they need a ride, or they need diapers, just selling their souls for $30." He said, "I'm the MAN, if they'll trust me, I'll do it. They don't need a sugar daddy, I'm the sugar daddy and I'll give them everything they need."

I responded, "Lord I'm not single, use one of those single sisters for that, I want my husband back." Still couldn't get over Darren Brown! How silly was that! Little did I know that God was talking about single sisters **all over the world!** I thought at the time, that He was talking about the parents at the daycare that I owned, but His vision for me was far greater. The whole purpose in me writing this book is for that very reason. So single sisters can know, that if they'll trust God and stop selling their souls to get their needs met, that He will do it for you and He'll do it far greater than what any sugar daddy can do for you. Not only that, but when He's doing it you won't feel used and abused. There won't be any guilt. You'll feel like the **Queen** that He created you to be! You'll have your dignity, your pureness and your swag! Because, He is the best provider! Sorry fellas, I don't mean to hate on your game but if your game's not right, she deserves better.

After another ten months go by, I get the same phone call that I had gotten ten months earlier. Darren calls and tells me to, "Take that truck back and buy the biggest one they have and get it brand new." I said, "WHAT! Daddy, do you know how much they want for that truck?" He said, "I know, people pay for what they want, take it back." I said, "I can't believe this I can't just keep taking cars back." He said, "You don't understand, you're a Queen! And you deserve the best, take it back and buy the new one. I don't want you driving a used car." I said, "No Daddy, you do that when you get home." I wasn't quite ready for that yet.

As time went on, one day I was driving down the street and saw this car go by. At that time, I thought that must've been the prettiest car I had ever seen. I said to myself, **"what is that?"** So, I followed the car until I could get close enough to see what it was. It was a soft powdered blue color, with rims, a sunroof, and all the works! That car must've been shining like new money that day. I said, "Lord I believe I ought to have me one of those." So, that Saturday I went to the dealership to test-drive one, but when I got there a brand new pearl white Lexus LX 470 was sitting at the door. I said "Oh Lord, there's that truck my husband told me to buy."

The salesman came up and I told him that I was there to test drive the LS, but my husband had told me a few months earlier to buy that LX. He said, "I'll tell you what, somebody is test driving the LS right now, so why don't you drive the truck until they get back." I said, "Okay." I got in that truck and fell in love. It was pearl on the outside, tan leather inside, every upgrade possible and **brand new!** I said, "Lord I came to look at that LS but this truck is 'all that'." I hadn't talked to my husband that day either, but when trying to decide which one to purchase I told the man I would be safe getting the LX since he had already told me to buy that one.

I'm only sharing these stories to show you how good God is and how if you seek ye first the kingdom and his righteousness all these things would be added. Read Matthew 6:33. Seeking the kingdom only means that He wants you to do things His way, there's nothing hard about that, and as you do, He rewards you with the good things that He wanted you to have in the first place. Jesus said that the Father already knows that you have need of these things. Sometimes we act like he doesn't, but he knows and he **will** provide. He is *Jehovah Jireh*. What I found out was, that I was able to accomplish far more with what I had than other people were able to accomplish with twice as much because I was seeking God's kingdom and His righteousness first. Obedience to God is what activates the power and favor of God to work in your life. In other words, I was able to possess the same things and not pay the same price.

Remember just a few years back, I was crying in that subdivision because I had no idea how I could enjoy that kind of life, but I kept walking with God and being faithful to Him and the blessings just started pouring in. If I had known then what I know now, I would've been laughing, not crying. I also believe that because I honored Darren in his absence that God honored me. I looked up one day and we were living the life that I had always dreamed of. It's just proof that God can turn **any** situation around for His glory if you cooperate with Him. Start letting God bless you! He wants to, you know? Most of the time it's our negative thinking that's hindering us, not God. As I said earlier, don't fear. Don't be afraid that things won't work out for you, because they will. Just train yourself to start listening to God so that He can tell you what it is you need to do to improve your life. He says He doesn't withhold any good thing from those who walk upright.

At this time, (maybe 9 or 10 years ago) I'm living in a beautiful home, own multiple cars, running a successful business and all because not only did I say 'YES' to God, but I also learned how to listen to Him.

Now, I'm not telling you to serve God so that He can make you rich, nor am I bragging by any means. What I'm telling you is that all that you're sacrificing yourself for, if you'll trust God and be obedient to Him, He'll provide it for you. Jesus said the Father already knows you have need of these things. That's why He tells you to seek the kingdom of God **first** and all of these **things** will be added unto you. What you don't understand is that it gives the Father good pleasure to give you the kingdom. He's excited about blessing you, He made all of these wonderful things for you to enjoy. He just wants to be first in your life, that's all. What I later realized is that GOD WAS SUSTAINING US FOR HIS OWN PURPOSE!

Chapter 7
How Do I Respect Him & Teach My Children To Respect Him?

When we went to visit Darren, he spent time with his children. We had Bible study together; he taught them scriptures and read them books. He talked to them about everything that was going on in their lives at home, at school and with their friends. He wanted to know it all and because of it, our children always connected with him. He was actually more involved in their lives in prison than most fathers who were present in the home.

I told you earlier that he always took care of the kids in spite of what he was doing, until he got really bad and would be gone all evening or all night. But even during those times, when he got home he immediately started to take care of them. He cooked for them, bathed them, ironed their clothes, got them ready for school and took them out with him most of the time. My mom used to say, "You don't keep those kids, Darren does." I said, "So what's the problem with that? They are *his* kids and I believe a father should raise his kids." Don't misunderstand; I wasn't negligent in any way, she was just bragging on Darren that day.

He took great pride in taking care of his children. Actually, he was a great caretaker to us all. It was something that he enjoyed doing. He had a very gentle and giving spirit. That's why it was so hard for us to be without him. My oldest daughter was his little princess. I believe that's why she took it the hardest. She wasn't able to comprehend what was going on. For five years she had her dad spoiling her rotten and without warning he was gone. You'll hear her thoughts on that later.

After he left, we kept the same rules in our house. Everybody had to ask Daddy for permission to do whatever he or she wanted to do. He still set the rules in our home and we abided by them. That was my way of making sure that he kept his dignity. I submitted myself to his authority as the Priest of our home, when I didn't have to. That helped to keep him going and it kept us connected. You have to realize that in prison, you don't control anything. Somebody tells you when to go to bed and when to get up, when you can watch T.V. and even when to eat. I just wanted my husband to feel like he still had control over something and that he was still important, not just another number. In other words I wanted him to have **HOPE!**

That was very important, because it determined how he behaved on a daily basis. He could've been killed on any given day in there based upon the way he handled situations. When you don't have anything to live for you may give up living. I didn't want that to happen to him, so I gave him the utmost respect and taught our children to do the same. As a result of how we handled the time in prison, it made it easier for us to adapt when he came home.

Now, there were certainly things we had to deal with when he came home, after all he had just spent 12 ½ long years in prison. There were some challenges it wasn't all easy. First, life was totally different for us on the outside than it had been when he left. Things as simple as using a cell phone was foreign to him because we didn't have cell phones when he went to prison. There are a lot of things that we take for granted because they're apart of our everyday life that people reentering society would have to adjust to when they've been gone for a long period of time.

God had blessed us and we were doing great! He came home to a beautiful family that loved and respected him, a beautiful home, and a thriving business. But as a man, he wanted to be the one who had provided these things for his family, so he had to battle with some insecurity. I had to help him see that God had in fact set it up for him to be successful. He had guided us all of those years so that he would make it when he got home. I reassured him that this wasn't something that he needed to feel insecure about. I reminded him of how we never could've accomplished what we accomplished if he hadn't been praying for us daily and giving me direction, which he had. I remember one day he told me "Just listen to me baby, I promise I'll never mislead you. I pray for my family everyday and God gives me direction for you. If you'll just listen to me and take heed, we'll be alright. I'll never lead you wrong." So that's what I did and we were alright.

Then because he hadn't been around women for 12 ½ years he was excited just looking at them. While I understood that, I wasn't almost going to accept anything but his faithfulness and loyalty to his children and me. That one didn't take long to realize, so other women were never an issue. He also had to deal with the shame and embarrassment of being in prison. He didn't want people to know he had been away and hated having to explain why he wasn't aware of how certain things worked in society, something he'd eventually overcome.

On top of the many things my husband had to overcome during his transition to the free world was anger. Prison makes you is angry. Boy, he would get upset over the simplest things when he first came home. I wasn't used to that because in spite of all that he did before he went to prison he was never mean. I would hear of people during that time that became mean or violent when they were using drugs but he never did. For some reason those characteristics were never there. He was always very gentle with me, even when I wasn't being gentle with him.

I would say, "What are you so angry about Daddy?" Maybe angry is a little strong, he wasn't angry or mean but very edgy, jumpy, and always ready to defend himself. All of our life together had been just the opposite. We got along so well that it was scary. He could tell me what I was thinking before I ever said a word. It was like he could feel me he shared my innermost thoughts. Then he explained to me how he always had to stay on guard in prison, just being around men all day everyday made him hard. Even if you were trying to do the right thing, in prison you always had to be concerned about what kind of day another person might be having. The simple things that we take for granted, like going to the restroom or taking a shower weren't so simple for him. Those are the most vulnerable times in prison because those are the times when somebody could attack you and you were the least prepared to defend yourself. It's a crazy world on the inside, and even though he didn't like it, he did have to adapt to it in order to survive.

Ladies, we're the soft side to men and when there are no women around, the part of him that is sensitive and caring then becomes hard and callous. Be patient though, he'll get it back, he just needs some nurturing. That's what you're there for. God gave them wives to help them, and depending on his need, determines the kind of help that you have to give. You have to adapt yourself to your husband.

A lot of men are good men they just need a woman who understands the male species, a woman who knows how to interact with him. Men need a woman who knows how to love the things that he needs *into* his life and the things that he doesn't need *out*. Wives, you are very powerful people. That's why God called you his **help**mate. You help him fulfill his God given purpose. This is not just for men who have been incarcerated but for any man.

Sometimes men are lacking certain traits needed to be a great husband or father or even a great man. The same thing goes for women. The key is not to use what you didn't get as an excuse for your behavior, but be willing to seek out the help you need to become a better person.

Never say, "that's just the way I am," always be willing to change if change is what's necessary to make things right. Your relationship should grow and develop as time goes on; it should never stay the same. You shouldn't be having the same problems five years into your marriage that you were having during the first six months. If you are, that simply means that somebody wasn't willing to change or neither of you was willing to change. That's a selfish attitude to have and it doesn't work well, not just when it comes to marital relationships but in any relationship. You probably have problems everywhere you go. Once again, what you have to realize is, that there are no perfect people in the world. You have to give room for grace in their lives. It's the same grace that you need, so always be willing to extend it to another person.

There were also adjustments that we had to make just living together again. Even though I had honored him as the head of our home while he was gone, there were still things that we both had to adjust to when it came to living together. We were almost like newlyweds in that arena. I didn't expect that because we had lived together for seven years before he left, so I thought it would be easy to pick up where we left off. In a lot of ways it was, but there were little things that we had to adapt to.

For instance, our first fight was on vacation. When he first came home we would drive down to Branson or the Lake of the Ozarks about once every five or six weeks just to spend some time alone and get to know each other again.

We couldn't go far because he was still on parole at the time. At any rate, the first time we took a trip, he wanted to lie around in the hotel room, relax, eat and watch T.V. the whole time away because he worked so hard while home. Well I wasn't used to that at all. When I took vacations they were to enjoy whatever city I was in. I wanted to do everything that the city had to offer. To me that was the whole point in going. But in his mind vacations were for getting rest! So we had this big fall out, so from then on, we decided that we would have **his** vacations and **my** vacations. If it was his vacation, we were going to rest but if it was my vacation we would be planning to do things all day long. That probably sounded real simple but when you're fighting, no matter how simple it starts, it can ruin a whole day or maybe even a week depending on how mature or immature you both are at the time.

Not too many other things mattered to me, I was so grateful to have him back in my life that anything he wanted I was willing to give. I still feel that way today. I look at him sometimes and just smile I'm so grateful to have him here. I wanted him back so badly and don't ever want to be without him again.

I had to stay prayerful for him because I didn't want him to fall back into trap. Even though he was strong in prison, I knew that he would be tempted beyond belief when he came home and he was! Can you imagine a wild animal being locked up for years? (I'm not calling men animals; I'm just trying to give you a mental picture). When somebody opens the cage; they're excited and overwhelmed about what's in front of them. They have options now; and are free to make their own choices. They are afraid of the unknown, yet eager to run buck wild. Women were looking at him as if he were fresh meat and didn't care if he was married or not, and not to mention old friends wanting him to get back into his old lifestyle. Now add all of that on top of the fact that he was still on parole for 5 years, coupled with still dealing with his own feelings of frustration. He was under a lot of pressure.

He was always extra respectful to people, thinking that he was still locked up and could be sent to the hole if he said or did what he really wanted to do. So sometimes I would say, "Daddy you're not in prison anymore, you don't have to act like that or you don't have to be afraid." It's a sad truth but prison is designed to rob you of your self-worth and to make you feel less than. It's really modern day slavery. If our young men would just stop falling into the trap, open their eyes and realize that they are KINGS, not slaves, the world would be a greater place.

Darren was released to a halfway house, where he had to work his way up to overnight stays at home. He hated it because he felt as though that wasn't true freedom. And though we had talked about it several times before while he was still in prison and I didn't agree, against my wishes, after a year and a half, he violated his parole and went back to prison. He was sentenced to 12 months and he would be completely free with no more parole.

Although I didn't want him to go that route, simply because I didn't want to be without him again, I realized later that it was the best thing to do. Believe it or not this was the first time since our wedding in 1986, and this was now 2007, that I wanted to leave him. When he called me and said that they were taking him back, I just lost it. I hung up the phone on him and would not remove the block off of my phone for him to call me back for about 3 days. Anybody who knew me, knew that Darren Brown and I were like peas and carrots. There was no separating us, so for me to block my phone for even a day was unbelievable. I was so disgusted with him because I had asked him not to do this, but his mind was made up and there wasn't any stopping him. He just felt like he couldn't go another day still in bondage. He would always say, "You can't be half free, either you're free or you're not and I'm not! I'd rather do this last little bit of time and get my life back then have to be on parole for another three and a half years."

I didn't feel like I could make it through another year of this prison life. It took all I could to make it through the last 15 years. I just thought to myself this is too much. I felt so strange because as I listened to myself talk, it didn't even sound like me. When I talked to my friends they were like, "what's wrong with you?" I knew I needed prayer and I knew I needed to pray, but I didn't feel like I could pray for myself at this time, I was just giving up. But just as God would have it, our church was having prayer that night for something, I don't even remember why now, but my friend and my sister prayed for me that night like never before.

Typically I was the one always doing the encouraging or praying for someone, or bailing them out financially, but that night I was totally dependent on their love for Darren to get us through. I said, "Lord, somebody has to pray that loves Darren, not just me. Because if it's just about me tonight I'm finished." Thank God for the power of prayer, and for people who know how to activate it. When prayer was over that night I was totally rejuvenated and felt like I could go on. I unblocked my phone so that he could call. He was having a panic attack because he had never experienced this before either, (being separated from me, not physically but emotionally). He was thinking that he didn't know what he was going to do without me. He was trying to make what he felt was the right decision for his family and for his family to be gone was more than he could bear. But I stood with him once again, we made it through those last twelve months but I never went to visit him. He decided that he didn't want to suffer through the visits again and that he could do this last bit of time easier if he didn't torment himself seeing us through the process. Then, when the twelve months were over we were able to go ahead and live our lives without somebody watching over him and having to report to somebody every week and still asking permission every time he wanted to do something. We couldn't even leave the city limits without permission, which once again kept him from being in control of his own family.

It's really a demeaning system, so try to have some understanding with your loved one who has had to experience this. I know it was probably their fault that they're in this situation, but still try to understand and have compassion. We've all made mistakes and done some things that we weren't proud of. Exercise patience! There will be some things that you learn during this process as well. I have encountered a lot of women over the years, who have no idea what they should expect when their loved one comes home from prison and because of it, they don't come home to the kind of environment that's necessary to help them stay out of prison and therefore, they end up going back. Sometimes they themselves don't even know what they need when they come home. They get here and try to figure out how to adapt.

My husband shared with me that often times when men have been locked up for a long period of time, they have this strong desire to have children when they get out. They want to leave a legacy if you please. The only problem with that is, because they are so excited over being around women again and having all kinds of choices, they usually end up sleeping with multiple women and having babies all over the city, some at the same time. And because they haven't properly prepared themselves to parent more children, then more children are born into fatherless homes. And a lot of times these same men become repeat offenders and go back to jail, possibly causing the cycle to repeat itself with his children, thereby leaving women and the government with the responsibility of caring for these babies. That's why ladies, you have to be accountable, somebody has to take responsibility for this. We'll talk about that later.

When I say it's a lot of pressure, believe me it's a lot. Try putting yourself in their shoes. They are probably unsure of how they're going to survive, especially if they can't find work. They may or may not have somebody who's willing to let them stay with them until they can get on their feet. They may have an opportunity to go to school or start a business if they have some kind of support system in place when they get home, but if not, they don't know how they're going to make it and can unfortunately return to a life of crime.

Prison is not some place you want to be and although I didn't want Darren to be in prison, initially that was because I didn't want him to be away from us. I hadn't thought about what being in prison was doing to him. It wasn't until he was moved to a facility in Colorado and we were there for a visit that I had a true epiphany about the effects of incarceration. We were out sightseeing after the visit and rode past a women's facility. My heart must have hit the floor because I guess subconsciously when I thought about prison, I only thought about men. To see a women's facility made me realize that it could've been me and I had never thought of that before. Not that I had committed a crime or anything, cause I hadn't, but it's a lot of innocent people in prison. That day I began to think about what it must be like for him in prison and I started to have compassion for him. I couldn't imagine having my freedom taken away from me, or being away from my children, not being able to hold my husband again, not being able to go where I want to go or do the things I like doing. Just the thought of it at the moment overwhelmed me, and I knew I never want to be in that predicament. My attitude changed after that. Not that I was doing anything wrong before, but I became conscious of doing things right.

I spoke very highly of Darren, before, during and after his imprisonment. I didn't allow people to talk bad about him or criticize him for what he had done, as a result, that helped his transition back into our extended family and our community. My take on that was, and still is, let he who is without sin, cast the first stone (John 8:7). And since nobody is without sin, I didn't see where any stones should be thrown. I acted like he had been there the whole time. I tried to be conscious at all times of what he might be feeling, so that I didn't do something that might agitate him during this process. Sort of like when you bring home a newborn baby from the hospital, you're extra careful with him/her, you're adjusting and so are they. Don't get me wrong I wasn't afraid of him or anything like that. He wasn't a violent person and, never had been. I was just trying to help his transition process, that's all. I knew being locked away from the rest of the world for one year, let alone sixteen years, with a bunch of men couldn't have been easy, so I was being mindful of his mental state.

Another thing I did, was to prepare our church family for his return. My church family was a huge part of my extended family and I needed him to be a part of that. Besides many of them had prayed and believed God with me for several years. This was a crucial part of his success. Having a strong support system was vital in him not returning to the life he once knew. He wasn't perfect, still isn't, neither am I or any of the rest of us, but he strives everyday to be more like Jesus and I'm extremely proud of his accomplishments! Darren has been home totally free for five years now and I thank God for the man of God He gave me. While he says to me, "nobody else would've waited 16 years for somebody to come home from prison baby", I say to him "and nobody else could've handled me." So we were in this thing together. I love him with all my heart. Our lives were good while he was away, but he told me over and over again, "our latter days would be far greater than our former." He would say "once we come together, I mean really together, there's no stopping us then. There's nothing that we can't have."

Sure enough, after he came home, God was faithful to his Word and our lives increased more. He immediately put his hands to the plow and made what we had better. For all of those people who said to me while he was gone, "I hope he appreciates you waiting on him" or "I hope he doesn't get home and mess up," I want you to know that his loyalty to me has been as admirable as my loyalty to him. He was definitely worth waiting for. I couldn't be happier. We're still on the rise because God recently told us that what we've been doing, what we have so far was only manna to us, this had nothing to do with where he was taking us. Manna is temporary substance; it's not permanent provision. It's what God provides until you get to the promise land! So promise land here we come!

Chapter 8

Your Children Are Affected by your Decisions

Realize that the decisions and choices you make impact your children. They will be a lot like you, so if you don't want your children doing what you're doing then maybe you should change. For example, you're sleeping with different men all the time, bringing all kinds of men/women around exposing them to things that they shouldn't be exposed to. You're drinking and getting high or you're allowing some man to beat on you. Is that what you want for your son or daughter? If your daughter watches you get abused, she may allow someone to abuse her when she's older. Or your son may be an abuser when he's older. We encounter a lot of youth who blame their parents for many of the issues in their life. Your children, even though they love you, won't respect you when they're older and that disrespect usually expresses itself in the form of rebellion. Like getting bad grades in school, not following the rules, being disrespectful in their conversations to name a few.

Another thing ladies, please don't dishonor your children by cussing in front of them or talking about adult situations in their presence. This causes them to grow up too fast. They hear about things that their young minds can't comprehend and don't know how to filter and they start repeating you. As a result you have two and three year olds who will curse you out, won't follow instructions and haven't been taught how to problem solve or express their emotions properly. You see, you're teaching your children at all times, it's just a matter of what you're teaching them. Children don't just grow up and become murderers, thieves, rapist or liars; they're on a path from birth. If you're not intentionally teaching your children to be respectful, if you're not setting boundaries and giving consequences for their actions, if you're not teaching them right from wrong and modeling the proper behavior in front of them, then you're setting them up for failure. In the same way its true that children don't just grow up and become doctors, lawyers, teachers, preachers or business owners either. Your children deserve to have parents who love, nurture and protect them; parents who educate them and train them to be successful members of society. Make life easier for your children not more difficult.

Stop sleeping around! There's a reason why God says to refrain from intercourse until you're married. There are a number of things wrong with it, but let's think about you sleeping with people you really don't even know. They could be crazy, a serial killer, have AID's, or any number of things. Anybody you lie down with could be a potential "BABY DADDY" and if he's crazy you could end up with crazy kids or kids you'll have to spend a lot of time in prayer over or casting off those hereditary spirits. We have enough to do as parents when they aren't crazy, we don't want to add to it by sleeping with people who wouldn't make great fathers. Even if they would make great fathers, don't set yourself up to be a single parent or set your child up to be raised in a single parent home when that can be avoided. Of course, there are extenuating circumstances. Maybe you're divorced or widowed, but if you were single when you laid down, then you were at risk of being a single parent. Don't create unnecessary trouble for yourself. Do it God's way, it really is the best way.

I know today some women feel like they don't even need a man to help raise their children. That's where we get artificial insemination amongst other things. That's how you feel, but that's not how that child will feel. They want to know and be around their father. You'll find out later when they're older how necessary he was. Women can't teach boys how to be men. After talking with my husband over the years I've come to understand that most men never had an example to live by or at least not a Godly one when it comes to being a husband, father, provider etc. Men have to be taught this skill and the fact that so many of them have not been taught, is the reason you believe now that you don't need a man to raise your child. You feel like you can do just as good by yourself, but that perpetual behavior is not going to change the problem we have in society today. You doing things differently will. You can teach your children a lot of things as their mother but you can't replace their father. He has a very specific, special and crucial God-given role to play in the lives of his children. A son needs his father to give him affirmation into manhood! Daughters need their fathers for protection and direction. She is taught what kind of man to say yes to from her father. Fathers are a very important part of the family structure. Statistics have already proven this, so I'm not telling you anything you don't already know.

A lot of women ask the question, "Should I wait?" Some of you are asking that question and your husband isn't in a physical prison. It gets hard sometimes I know. You see all that I went through and the end results were well worth it for me, but that's not everybody's story. Neither is it the will of God for everybody to wait. The best thing that I can leave with you is to be led by the Holy Spirit. He's your Teacher and he's your Friend. He'll tell you what's right for you and your situation. Learn to pray and listen to that still small voice on the inside. He'll direct you in the way in which you should go. (Isaiah 48:17) Know this though, I've already said this once, if you're with an abusive man, don't waste your time praying. GET OUT NOW! At least until he's been delivered from his abusive behavior. In the meantime love him from afar. Don't ever allow yourself to be in an abusive relationship. God's not asking you to do that. You don't have to stay for the children's sake. I say that because so many women in abusive relationships think that they need to stay for their children. In actuality you're doing more harm to your children than good by staying, because you're exposing them to an unhealthy environment. It's better that they not be around their father at all, than to watch him abuse you and possibly them to.

Now imagine this. Women all over the world start saying "NO! Not until we're married!" You see, most of the problems women have with men are the result of our own tolerance. Men couldn't cheat if other women weren't there for them to cheat with. Start respecting not only other women, but respect yourself as well. The world will be a much better place when we wake up and take back the respect and honor that's been lost. I know some people don't believe it's possible, but if every woman reading this book changes her mind, then men are forced to change the way they treat you. If everybody says no, then men will start marrying you and not using you, because they won't be able to.

Husbands will be faithful to their wives because there won't be any body to cheat with. If you don't believe it's possible, then how about just starting with you? You make the change first and see if it works for you, like it did for me. My husband treats me like a queen because that's where my tolerance level is. You don't have to accept treatment that's less than your expectations. Make sure that your expectations are realistic though. Don't expect a man that never makes mistakes, because there are none. Just like you can't be a woman that never makes mistakes. What I'm saying is have STANDARDS. Be the best woman that you can be, so that a man will want to be the best man that he can be for you. Get rid of the list of men who have had the opportunity to say that they've been with you. You're a jewel, save yourself for your husband and when he gets you, he'll be getting a prize. It's not a prize if everybody else has already used it. Nobody goes to the store to buy used shoes or clothing. If they do it's at the thrift store and there you don't expect to pay full price. In other words, used clothing doesn't get the same respect as new clothing, because it doesn't have the same value.

Some of you reading this book, say well Mrs. Tonya, it's too late for me I'm not a virgin. That's okay; the good thing about God is that, all you have to do is repent (have a change of heart) and start living right now. It's not too late. Don't yield to that "might as well syndrome." That's when girls say; I've already messed up so I might as well go ahead and stay in this relationship. No! You shouldn't, even if you're in a lesbian relationship or you're involved in prostitution, it's still not too late to repent. Most of the time women only get into ungodly relationships because they're hurting or they're lost and trying to find themselves. God loves you and will accept you back no matter what you've done. He hates sin but he loves the sinner. Take a chance and see what GREAT things God has in store for you.

Look at John 4:1-42, this is a story about a woman who had been with many men and wasn't married to the man she was currently with. What's so profound about it is that she was the first woman that Jesus revealed Himself to and turned her into a preacher of the gospel. After meeting Jesus that day she went and won a great portion of her town to Christ. Can you imagine that, the whole town listening to what you have to say? If He used her, then certainly He can use you.

Chapter 9

Misplaced Love

Listen ladies you might as well bow down and call him Lord, because he has certainly become your god. Now there is a time when we should call our husbands Lord, like Sarah called Abraham her Lord, read 1 Peter 3:6 that I shared with you earlier. But what she was doing was acknowledging him as the priest, the head of the family. She was honoring his kingship. He is the king under the KING OF KING (JESUS). See, if you're obeying a man over the Word of God, you have distorted his position in your life and made him your god. Those situations usually end up with some unnecessary sufferings, be it now or later. When I was sleeping with Darren but God had asked me to keep myself and I thought I couldn't do it, there came a time when I had to do just that and it was for far longer than it would've been if I had just obeyed him earlier. Remember, God is not trying to keep anything good from you. He's only trying to get you to His best.

Let's get rid of the spirit of greed as well. For some of you it's not the man that's the problem. You're greedy and you want more than what you have prepared yourself for, so you'll sell yourself cheap to get it and sometimes even sell your soul. Now, I told you how I wanted a better life for my children and there's nothing wrong with that, everyone should. It only becomes a problem when you don't want to exercise patience and wait on God to show you how to get it, or if you're lazy and you don't want to work yourself to get what you want. The Bible says in Proverbs 14:23 in the NIV that *all hard work brings a profit.* If you'll work hard it **will** pay off, as long as you stick with it. Don't quit before you are rewarded. It also says in Proverbs 28:19 in the NCV

> *"Those who work their land will have plenty of food, but the ones who chase empty dreams instead will end up poor."*

Now, if you're lazy and don't want to work for yourself but would rather use your body to get your needs met than put this book down until you're ready to change. I'm not trying to be hard on you don't misunderstand me. I'm simply saying that knowledge with no intent to apply does you no good. By lazy, I mean that you don't want to go to school or work extra hours or spend time researching out ideas or even spending time in prayer so God can speak to you. Be willing to do whatever it takes to improve your standard of living without compromising yourself or your integrity.

Another problem is accountability. We lie down and have these babies but we want other people to be responsible for them. By other people I mean we want to receive government assistance or we want other men to volunteer their time with our kids or we want people to feel sorry for us and give us a handout because we're a single parent. Now of course not all single parents feel this way, so if this doesn't apply to you, just share it with someone else who may be able to benefit from it. But I've met many single mothers over the years who expect that other people should sacrifice their time and money to ensure their child's well being when that is solely your responsibility. You want to make outsiders accountable when you won't even hold the people responsible for these children accountable and that's you and their father. Why should other people be responsible to pick up your slack? Like

I stated earlier, there could be a number of reasons why you're a single parent so this may not apply to you at all. But if you were single when you laid down then that's why you're a single parent. Therefore you have to be accountable for your choices and the decisions you've made. Don't get me wrong, I don't mind helping people and giving out of my overflow and I do all the time. I'm simply trying to get you to see where you may have gone wrong so that you can change your thought process. Not blaming anybody else, not even his or her father because unless you were abused, you chose to lie down with him.

What I'm saying is this. You need to do some preventive maintenance. Think about who you're sleeping with before you sleep with him. If you go out to the club tonight, meet someone and decide to go to bed with him that was your choice. But if you get pregnant by him and have no idea what kind of person he really is, why would that be the rest of the world's responsibility to step in and help you out? If it was your choice then it is YOUR responsibility. Not your mother's or your friends' or other people in the community, and not even the government. Although there may be times that you need help, and that's okay, just know that ultimately your children are your responsibility.

When Darren went to prison I didn't look for anybody to feel sorry for me or to give me a handout. I didn't think it was fair for other people to have to take from their household to support mine, so I figured I better find a way to make it work and with the help of God I did. I received food stamps for those 9 months that I told you about earlier when I quit my job, but I felt so uncomfortable the whole time that I knew I was going to have to do something different. Besides that, when I quit my job one organization offered me help but then didn't give it to me, so I never expected anyone to help me again. I'm saying all of this to say, as you're realizing your worth, realize it in every area of your life.

Have some good Godly pride about you. Stand up and take charge of you and your children's lives by making you a better you. Now, if you're receiving state assistance don't beat yourself up over it, I'm not trying to condemn you. Use it to get yourself to a better place. Find out what you're good at, go back to school and pursue a career. Train your children to be hard workers. Find out what they're good at and help them perfect their gift so that they are living a life of purpose and not wandering around for 20-30 years frustrated and causing trouble because they don't know what they should be doing.

Sacrifice your time and energy investing in your child. Help them with their homework, make sure that they are learning don't assume that they are. Teach them to be respectful and productive. Share your past challenges with your children so that they can learn and grow from the wisdom you've attained. Guide, instruct and train your children so that you receive the desired outcome from them (productive, self sufficient citizens in society).

For some of you reading this book, it hasn't been easy for you, because maybe you've become promiscuous because you were raped or molested by a perverted uncle, cousin or step-father and maybe even could've been killed during the process or maybe abandoned and your heart hurts. Maybe your mother was like that and you've taken on her spirit. You've tried to move on but you can't let go of the pain or the shame. You feel nasty and ugly and you blame yourself somehow for what happened to you, but it wasn't your fault and it isn't your fault. Whatever the reason you find yourself in this low state you can be free from that today as well.

With God's ability in you, you can overcome every circumstance and every stronghold of the enemy. You see when Jesus gave you the keys to the kingdom (Matthew 16:19), He said that you had power to bind and loose. He said, "whatever you bind on earth would be bound in heaven and whatever you loose on earth would be loosed in heaven." In other words, whatever you allow, He will allow, but if you don't allow it you have all of heaven backing you up. You have authority over circumstances you don't have to be bound by them. Say this right now,

"Father, in the name of Jesus, I release this shame and guilt and this heavy load I've been carrying back to you. You told me to cast my cares on you because you cared about me. Now I release these feelings in exchange for your joy, beauty and restoration. I release the person/people who hurt me and robbed me of my innocence. I also forgive myself of any past mistakes. Today I become brand new again in you. In the name of Jesus, I take authority

over this promiscuous spirit and I command it to get off of me, never to operate in my life or the life of my children and my children's children after me ever again! Thank you for new opportunities and new vision and for giving my life purpose. Begin to use my issues for your glory, help me to help someone else overcome because no matter what the circumstance "I WIN". This did not defeat me but only gave me an opportunity to be an instrument that you can use to help change somebody else's life. I am free to live my life in a manner that's pleasing before the Lord. I'm not a slave to sin anymore!" In Jesus' name, Amen.

Paul states in Romans 6:16 NCV,

> **"Surely you know that when you give yourselves like slaves to obey someone, then you are really slaves of that person. The person you obey is your master. You can follow sin which brings spiritual death or you can obey God, which makes you right with Him."**

I had plenty of opportunities in those 16 years to do other things. There were men who would've gladly taken care of my children and me.

I had plenty of offers, but I wasn't interested. I chose to keep myself and wait on God to bless me and because I did it God's way I wasn't left feeling cheap or embarrassed or having to sneak around and lie to get what I wanted. Also remember, I told you earlier that I hadn't prepared myself for the kind of life I wanted either that's why I was crying out to God, so I'm not trying to judge you by any means, I'm only trying to show you a better way.

The one thing I don't want you to do is become offended with me. If you allow yourself to become offended, then you won't be able to hear me and my whole purpose in writing this book is to help you change your life for the better not to hurt you in any way. Remember, God loves you and I'm writing this book in the Love of God, not to condemn you or make you feel bad. So, if you find yourself somewhere in this book, don't get angry, at least not at me, get angry at the devil who's been tricking you out of your BEST life and let's change! I can hear some of you saying, Mrs. Tonya, you didn't always get treated like a queen. You had to go through some things too. I know that, that's why once again I'm pleading with you to go a different route. God wants to take you further than you've ever dreamed or imagined, but He has to have your cooperation. If you've never accepted Christ into your heart, let's do that now. It's real simple. Romans 10:9-10 NCV says,

> 9 *"If you use your mouth to say 'Jesus is Lord,' and if you believe in your heart that God raised Jesus from the dead, you will be saved. 10 We believe with our hearts, and so we are made right with God. And we use our mouths to say that we believe, and so we are saved."*

So all you have to do to become a part of God's family is believe that Jesus Christ is the son of God and that God raised him from the dead for your sins. Then of course, confess that with your mouth.

There is no other way. I know many people believe that there are multiple ways to get to God, but that's simply not the truth. You see God sent Jesus to die for you in order to pay the price for your sins. Jesus is God's total plan of salvation for you. If you reject Jesus you reject God's plan, there is no other way.

Think about it this way, if I told you to come to my house Saturday at 6:00pm with my daughter for this Grand feast and you got all excited, and began going around telling everyone that you're coming to my house on Saturday at 6:00pm, but that you weren't coming with my daughter. Furthermore, you don't even like my daughter, but you believe that I'll let you come over anyway. Now, it's also true that you believe that, it's true that you're sharing with everybody that you're coming to my house, but the fact of the matter is, when you get to my house on Saturday at 6:00pm you **won't** get in. Do you honestly believe that I'm going to prepare this Grand feast and have you over to share my wealth with me and you don't even like my child? If you don't like her, you don't like me. You can forget it, and when you get to my house not only will you not get in but I would probably call the police on you and have you taken away for trespassing. That's how it is with God. You can't get to him if you don't honor His Son. 1Timothy 2:5-6 NCV says,

> 5 *"There is one God and one way human beings can reach God. That way is through Christ Jesus, who is himself*

human. 6 He gave himself as a payment to free all people. He is proof that came at the right time."

Maybe you don't know why you are the way you are or why you act the way you act. Maybe you're going to have to take some time to get to know who you are. Maybe it's time to look deep inside yourself to answer some of the questions you may have. Once you know the (whys) then you can resolve the issues, because you've gotten to the root of the problem.

I didn't have any intention of bombarding you with scriptures when I sat down to write this book, but I am trying to help you get out of your current situation and the Word of God never fails. I tried to help you see through my own life's example how your relationship with Christ is what helps you to understand your own self worth. YOU ARE A QUEEN and you're a part of a royal kingdom, so start treating yourself like it! When I was going through this time of Darren's drug use and imprisonment, I appreciated the books I read that gave scripture references because they helped me to know how to apply the Word of God to my life. So I hope this was helpful to you and not burdensome or hard to understand. In this time that we live in now, a lot of people live their lives like there is no God or like our decisions now don't impact our eternal life, but they do.

It's therefore wise to find out what God expects of us, so that we can make the right decisions now while we still have a chance. That's what getting to know him is all about. You agree that the more you get to know someone the easier it becomes to please him or her. Well, two things happen when we start to spend time with God. 1. You begin to find out who God is, how he thinks, how he acts, what he likes and what he doesn't like. As a result you know what to expect from him and what he expects from you. 2. You begin to find out who you are.

Now, finding out who God is, 'WOW', now that's exciting. To see how good He is and how much He loves you and all that he's done for you. But finding out who you are, well, that may not feel so good. A lot of times we don't even want to know who we really are because in our fallen state we can look pretty ugly. We can act ugly, curse people out, lie, manipulate, cheat, be full of anger, envy and jealousy. We can find all kinds of evil when we look at ourselves, like un-forgiveness and the list goes on. But the good thing about finding out who you are is, 1. You begin to understand and appreciate the grace of God better. 2. You don't have to stay that way. You can begin to change who you are by fellowshipping with who God is.

Lastly let me say this, you don't know what you don't know until you learn it. So everyday we're living out as much as we know, but you may still be acting ignorantly in some areas of your life because you have yet to be enlightened in that area. Then sometimes you realize after time goes by that you're not even living out the revelation that you once walked in and you have to go back and remind yourself.

Sometimes you are your own encouragement. Instead of hearing about what God has done for somebody else to be encouraged, you start reminding yourself about all that He's done for you and how faithful He's been to you. Build yourself up on your most Holy Faith, praying in the Holy Spirit according to Jude 20. As you're praying in the Holy Spirit (in tongues) and I know some people don't believe in that, but it is the will of God for you to be filled with the Spirit with the evidence of speaking in other tongues. (Acts 2:4) So as you're praying in the Holy Spirit he'll begin to bring things up out of you. He'll bring back to your remembrance scriptures that you've forgotten, victories, challenges that you've overcome. See, you're building **yourself up** there are only victories for you, never defeat. If something's not working out for you don't panic, Philippians 4:6-7 NIV says,

> *6 "Do not be anxious about anything, but in every situation, by prayer and petition, with thanksgiving, present your requests to God. 7 And the peace of God, which transcends all understanding, will guard your hearts and your minds in Christ Jesus."*

Maybe it's not working out because that's not God's perfect plan for you. See He's always trying to protect you and give you His best. He's never withholding anything good from you, read Psalm 84:11.

This happened to me once and I made a major mistake in my life. I wanted to buy a new home. I had searched for several months, and looked at who knows how many properties; when lo and behold, I found the perfect house. It had everything I wanted, everything I told God I wanted to put in my house when I bought it, was already there. I talked to my husband, him still being in prison at the time, and told him all about it. I showed him pictures and asked for his permission to buy this property. Initially he was a little hesitant, but later he agreed, so I began the process of purchasing this house. All kinds of things kept happening and eventually my husband told me he felt that we needed to back out of this deal because he didn't feel that this was God. He said, "I know what I said before, but something's just not right about this, it's too many different obstacles. The blessings of the Lord maketh one rich and addeth no sorrow with it, there's too much sorrow with this." But I said, "nooooo Daddy, this house is perfect and the devil's not going to stop me from having God's best." This is where you have to be careful. There's a difference between the obstacles that the enemy puts in your way trying to stop you, and the closed doors that God puts there to protect you. The way to know the difference is back to Philippians 4:6. Don't be anxious and determined to have your own way then you can clearly hear what God is saying to you.

Now during this process I must've said 100 times, literally, that I could build this house for a little more than half of what I'm paying for it, but in all the times that I said it, it never occurred to me that that was the voice of God **telling** me to build the house. I was so determined to have **that** house that I couldn't hear anything else. You know how you finally find what you've been looking for and you're thinking that if you let this go, you may never get it back again. That's what I must have been thinking, that and being impatient, or why else wouldn't I have just taken the time to build the house.

I wanted it and I wanted it NOW! I eventually had to foreclose on that property because what the rest of the world just experienced a few years ago, I experienced it then. After we bought the house we couldn't get the appraised value out of it, it was coming up way short. We went through all sorts of things with that property and I remember Darren saying to me "If you don't pack your bags and get out of that house and stop acting like God stopped making houses when he made that one! You'll find another house." It took me a long time to accept that, but I finally came to the realization that God wasn't in it and that I was wasting my time and energy trying to keep it. The funny thing is it sold after I foreclosed on it, for exactly what I said I could build it for.

God had even tried to save me again before I purchased the house. The seller had put two contracts on the property and the other buyer put a lien against the property so that when they went to record it at the courthouse they couldn't. We had to get attorney's to represent all parties and during this process. He told me that he even offered me money to let him buy the house. So I said, "Oh yea, well how much did he offer me?" He said, "$25,000". I said, "Well why didn't you tell me that before?" He said, "Because I didn't think you cared about the money, I thought you only wanted the house." And the truth of the matter is, he was right. Anyway a few days later when we were all to meet, I said, "Lord if he'll offer me $50,000 I'll take it and fix up the daycare and build the house somewhere else."

Well, we get to the meeting, the guy's attorney meets with me separately, offers me $50,000 and I turn it down. I know you're thinking to yourself right now, what in the world was wrong with her? She couldn't be that stupid or blind, but how many of you right now are in similar situations and don't even realize it. It may not be with a house, maybe your house is a job offer or a car or that boyfriend you won't let go of, that God keeps warning you about. I know it seems to you that this was too obvious for me to miss, but I missed it nonetheless. Your situation is obvious too, to everyone else around you. You're the only one who can't see clearly what God is saying to you. But stop now before you make a mistake that could cost you for years to come, like I did.   You see, not only did I pay with my credit, but also it crushed me spiritually for a long time missing it to such a huge magnitude that way. It took me a long time to recover. I felt like I had been demoted from my place of authority and I had to work my way back up. Some of this was just the lies of the enemy that I wasn't casting down and some of it was me proving myself again.

Like at your company for instance, if you're in a top position and you blow a huge account, the boss is not just going to give you another one right away. You have to take some time to show what you've learned from your mistakes and what led up to the mistake and how you can keep you from making the same mistake again. You even have to show how it can work to the company's advantage if they'll trust you again. That's how I was spiritually. I was proving myself again, not only to be restored back into my position, but to be promoted to an even higher place. And because God is so faithful, guess what? He promoted me.

Now search your heart and life and make sure that you're not on the verge of some life altering decision. Don't be anxious, exercise patience. In other words, calm down and listen to what God is saying to you. If you make that a practice, you'll always come out on top! Take time to listen, don't be in such a hurry like I was, then you won't have to spend valuable time, that you could be using to further your dreams, recovering the losses.

Now I want to say something to the woman who has sat down and read this entire book and says Mrs. Tonya what you've said is good for all of those women dealing with their husband, boyfriend, son or whoever their loved one is but what about me? I'm the one in prison, or I'm the one on drugs. Maybe your children have been taken away from you by the authorities or by a caring grandparent or other relative and you want your life back. Well, I have good news for you. TODAY IS YOUR DAY! As I have impressed on you all throughout this story, there's nothing too hard for God. I want you to pray this prayer and not only are you going to be free from the chains that have held you bound but you're going to get your child(ren) back as well. You'll be given another opportunity to be the GREAT mom that I know you are and that God has called you to be. Say this,

"Father in the name of Jesus, I'm coming to you now asking you to forgive me of all my shortcomings. You said that if I would confess my sins that you would be faithful and just not only to forgive me but to cleanse me from all unrighteousness. I thank you that while I'm releasing all of these bad habits to you that you are releasing your grace to me. I thank you that because

you are a God of another chance, that you are affording me another opportunity to do this right. I can do all things through Christ who strengthens me and with your strength I can say no to _____. You no longer have control over me. The blood of Jesus has washed me clean. I am a great mother and I'm taking my children back now! I thank you for mending my relationship with my children and my family. I thank you in advance that you have already prepared the way for me and you are ordering my steps so that I may quickly obtain employment to provide for me and my children that I may not be dependent upon anyone but you Lord. Satan I come against your plan to destroy my life and to bring division between my children and me. Jesus said that he came to destroy the works of the devil and I agree with him that your works are destroyed in my life. I thank you this day Father for redemption and restoration. It's in your son Jesus' name that I pray Amen!"

Now that God has given you another chance at life, go and make the most of it. Hold your head up high and proudly take your life back. Ask your children to forgive you and you forgive yourself. Don't waddle in the mud another minute, you are brand new and you are forgiven! Others may try to condemn you and remind you of your past. Don't be discouraged by that, trust has to be restored. You just keep moving forward, making the healthy choices for you and your family. You're probably asking yourself, if it's that easy? Yes it is! The power of God is real and he can deliver you instantly. All you need to do is believe he can do it. (Matthew 9:27-29) says,

> *27 "When Jesus was leaving there, two blind men followed him. They cried out, "Have mercy on us, Son of David!" 28 After Jesus went inside, the blind men went with him. He asked the men, "Do you believe that I can make you see again?" They answered, "Yes, Lord." 29 Then Jesus touched their eyes and said, "Because you believe I can make you see again, IT WILL HAPPEN!"*

Chapter 10

Teen Section

Have you ever been in love? A lot of times that's where our troubles begin as teenagers. We open ourselves up to a lot of pain and unnecessary hardship by getting involved in relationships that we're much too young for. Our emotions are not ready for the kind of pressures and disappointment that those kinds of relationships bring, and as a result we began to lose sight of ourselves, who we are and what we're capable of. So instead of realizing how smart and beautiful we are, we start feeling less than or not good enough. You are young, you're beautiful, you're smart, but he's telling you otherwise. Maybe not with his words but maybe he's cheating on you, maybe abusing you physically or trying to control you. He's causing you to have low self-esteem, maybe even identity issues, where now you think you like girls instead. Or maybe the devil's lying to you saying you may as well get with a girl, she won't mistreat you like the boys do, she'll understand you better. So you get caught up in more bad relationships, the kind God never intended for you.

Lesbianism is immoral just like fornication and God didn't make you that way. He doesn't go against His own will. If He did He wouldn't be fair and just. There are spirits that carry themselves from generation to generation looking for a person to dwell in until somebody breaks free by renewing their mind with the Word of God and releasing your family from that curse.

If you look at your family tree you'll probably find that somebody in the generation right before you and no further than two generations back struggled with the same spirit. There are other ways this spirit could've entered in as well. You may have been molested by a man or a woman or seen some things on T.V. that you shouldn't have seen or maybe a friend introduced you to it. However it got in, you have to get it out. There are a lot of things that you may want to do that aren't right, but the reason you don't follow through with them is because somewhere along the line you were taught that they weren't appropriate so you had a change of mind. It's the same thing with being a lesbian, instead of agreeing with it, realize that it's not appropriate and allow the Word of God to change your mind. 1 Thessalonians 4:3-8 NCV says,

3 "God wants you to be holy and to stay away from sexual sins. 4 He wants each of you to learn to control your own body in a way that is holy and honorable. 5 Don't use your body for sexual sin like the people who do not know God. 6 Also, do not wrong or cheat another Christian in this way. The Lord will punish people who do those things as we have already told you and warned you. 7 God called us to be holy and does not want us to live in sin. 8 So the person who refuses to obey this teaching is disobeying God, not simply a human teaching. And God is the one who gives us his Holy Spirit."

Also Romans 1:26-27 states,

26 "Because people did those things, God left them and let them do the shameful things they wanted to do. Women stopped having natural sex and started having sex with other women. 27 In the same way, men stopped having

natural sex and began wanting each other. Men did shameful things with other men, and in their bodies they received the punishment for those wrongs. "

So you see, God is not pleased with that behavior and I know in your heart you really want to please God. Maybe you didn't know what God said about it but now that you've been enlightened, choose the right path.

College campuses are breeding grounds for these immoral spirits. It's usually where girls start to come out. Those spirits are strong on the campuses because there are so many young people there anxious to explore the world with no supervision and no boundaries except the ones that they set for themselves. But now even in high school and some elementary school age girls are being bombarded with this spirit. Don't yield to peer pressure and remember the things that you were taught by your parents or guardians. Follow their teaching, if they were good instructors. That will help to keep you safe. You have to resist it and be free, not agree with it. It is NOT okay for you to sleep with other women, that's perversion and it's not God's will for your life.

You're right when you say it's your choice, everything in life is about choices; it's just not the right one. Somehow people have misconstrued the love of God with his acceptance for their rebellious ways. God's word declares that nothing can separate us from the Love of God which is in Christ Jesus. That's true that we can't be separated from it, but that doesn't keep us from reaping the consequences from the seeds that we've sown. Remember once again, that God loves you with an unconditional love and He only wants you to experience His best.

Now back to the boys, some of you don't even realize that he's the problem. Your relationship with him is what's causing you to do badly in school or disobey your parents because you're sneaking around trying to be with him when you should be in class or at home. One thing about young girls having sex, is that they then began to think they're grown and don't want anybody telling them what to do, especially their parents. But you have to honor your parents if you want to receive God's best in your life. That's what I mean by him causing you trouble. You're much too young to take on these kinds of emotions, so please, please, please wait until you are of age.

Maybe that's not your situation at all, maybe your problems stem from within your own home. Maybe your parents' were/are abusive or neglectful. Maybe you've had to try and fend for yourself because of neglect, so you're selling yourself cheap because you don't know what else to do to survive. Maybe your father wasn't or isn't there to tell or show you how much he loves you, so you're looking for love in all the wrong places. You start doing things just to be doing it, without even knowing or understanding why, allowing yourself to be used. Just another notch on his belt is all he's trying to accomplish, but you have to realize yourself worth. Began to understand that God took his time and formed you, made you all special and beautiful and you have power on the inside of you to conquer the world. Remember when you give him your virginity you're giving him all of you. Save it for the person that God has planned for your destiny, don't waste yourself on people just passing through. You're worth so much more than that.

If you were robbed of your virginity, meaning if you were raped or molested, you can still be clean again, pure in the sight of God. Don't take on the title of victim and just start abusing and disrespecting yourself because somebody else disrespected you. Take back what they stole from you however hard that might be. Forgive this person because they have no idea what kind of pain they have caused you. For them to do to you what they've done means they're sick, they need some help, so pray for them. Let's do that right now.

"Father in the name of Jesus, I come to you today first off thanking you that in spite of all the things that have happened to me, I'm still here. And because I'm still here means that I'm an over comer, you've given me another chance to do something great. I forgive the person/people who hurt me and I'm asking you to help them as well. I release all of the hurt from my past and will do everything I can to make my life count. I thank you for healing my family and me and turning this tragic situation into something that can be used to help others. Help me to start over today fresh and anew. I choose today to forget about the things in my past and I look forward to the great future that's ahead of me. Father I thank you that as I release the guilt hurt and

shame of my past that I am once again pure in your sight. I thank you for the ability to love myself again, and because I love myself I won't abuse me or allow others to use me for their pleasure. I thank you for the awesome plan you have for me and I receive it now in Jesus' name Amen!"

Don't make the mistakes that I made as a teenager. Spend this time focusing on your education. Have fun, laugh and enjoy life. Don't complicate your life by getting involved in intimate relationships. Trust me you'll have plenty of time for that when you're older and can understand better how to handle it.

Find something that you can do. What are you good at? Find a way to give back. Stop making life all about you and figure out how you can help somebody else young or old. You can always make better decisions when you aren't being self-centered because then you take time to think. Maybe you're good at doing hair or teaching young children how to read. Maybe you're a good listener and you could be good company for your grandmother or an elder at the nursing home. Whatever your gifts and talents are they could be used to help encourage somebody else and to keep you out of trouble. Spend your time and energy focusing on things that are helpful and healthy for you and less time trying to figure out how you can get a boyfriend. You'll be glad you did. And be sure to take heed to the advice of your guardian, rather it is your mother, father, grandmother, aunt or whoever is raising you. Make it a practice to listen to them and respect them. God will bless you for it.

Let me just leave you with this one piece of advice. Don't live the rest of your life not able to flourish and grow and bring out all of the beautiful gifts that are in you because you're blaming your parents for what they did or didn't do. It may not seem fair but allow God to do something great in you, in spite of not having everything or everybody that **you** thought you needed. Remember your life didn't catch God by surprise and everything and everybody you needed to fulfill HIS plan, you had it!

Final Thoughts

One thing that helped me through all of this was realizing that I wasn't the only one going through this. You see a lot of times the enemy will try to discourage you and isolate you by telling you a bunch of lies, building a wall of shame when you don't have anything to be ashamed of. Everybody has a cross to bear and even though your friend or neighbor may not be dealing with the same thing, he's telling them the same lies because that's what he does. He lies to everybody. Jesus called him the father of lies, He said he had been lying since the beginning. All he knows how to do is lie. Our responsibility in that is not to listen to it. God told us in (2 Corinthians 10:3-5) that we weren't fighting the same way the world fights. You see our weapons have power to destroy the enemy's strong places. We cast down every thought that exhalteth itself above the knowledge of God and bring it captive and make it obey Christ. In other words we control our thoughts because our thoughts run our life (Proverbs 4:23). You can't allow yourself to just think about anything, or let your thoughts run wild. If you don't control them, the enemy will have you hating people without a cause, your mate and anybody else that you're around. He causes envy, jealousy, back biting and lying because he's evil and so are all of his deeds. So think about things that are pure and lovely and of a good report, if there be anything trustworthy be any praise, think on these things (Philippians 4:8).

Know that whatever your circumstance you can rest in the fact that God has your back. Don't be nervous, don't panic because things are not going the way you want them to right now. It's just another opportunity for you to draw closer to God. Stop and ask him, "Okay Lord, what do you want me to do now? How do I get out of this situation and turn it around?" You see it's been given you to know the secrets of the kingdom; Luke 8:10. You can't be trapped or snared, you have the Holy Spirit living on the inside of you and he'll always direct you if you let him.

There's nothing hard about walking with God, so stop telling yourself that it is. The key is you have to stop wanting your own way and want His. Be like Jesus, He said "not my will but thy will be done;" Mark 14:36. Get to a place in your life where, it's Lord I just want what you want for me. Nothing more, nothing less and you'll find that that's a great place to be because God wants far more for you than you could ever imagine. When I quit my job, I just believed God to replace my income. I had no idea how God really wanted to bless me and even more so now because it's not over for me yet; it's only just beginning. I remember when Darren first got sentenced I thought that life would be over by the time he got home. At 27 years old I couldn't fathom what life would be like in 15 years. All I could think about is everything that I knew I needed him for and wanted him to be a part of; he wasn't going to be there for.

Everyone wants the perfect love story with a happy ending and you **can** have that. Just allow God to give it to you his way. It's much less painful. Let me reiterate one last time some thoughts I shared with you earlier. Men have needs, but it's not your responsibility to satisfy them, if you're not his wife. A man merely saying I love you means nothing. A man telling you that he loves you doesn't warrant you giving him all of you, even if he really believes that he means it at the time.

If you don't get the commitment it will still end up in heartbreak sooner or later. **You have to be convinced that you are worth the wait!** Then you can convince him that you're worth it. Wait until the ring is on your finger and you've said "I do" before the man of God, otherwise he'll be satisfied but you won't.

I'll say again that they will tell you whatever it is you want to hear to conquer you. It doesn't matter that they don't mean it; they'll still say it. If he tells you that you are too much work, tell him "thank you" and keep it moving. That only meant that you were a notch in his belt that he didn't get. When a man really wants you and wants you for keeps, he won't stop until he gets you.

You hold the keys to your future ladies, not him. Don't ever act out of desperation, take your time and choose wisely. This is your life we're talking about, not a pair of shoes. Get to know all sides of him, because men are very good at only showing you what they want you to see, especially when they're on a "mission to conquer." Make sure he's not an abuser rather that is physically, mentally, emotionally or verbally. Remember this; men want women that they can respect. Don't be deceived into believing that you have to be loose in order to get a man. You don't just want **A** man, you want **THE** man God has designed specifically for you. You want the man who wants you and can't do without you, not the one you think you want. And lastly, always, always, always be led by the Holy Spirit and remember to study your word so that you'll know what God expects from you. That's the only way to know how to live.

A Daughter's Perspective

For the person reading this book that has a husband or boyfriend in prison and especially to the young girl whose father is in prison. My daughter wrote a small segment sharing the sentiments of her heart of what having a father in prison was like for her growing up. She shares this in hopes that if you're a mother with a daughter whose father is in prison you can gain some insight into how your daughter might be feeling and if you're the little girl who has lost her father to imprisonment, you can gain hope knowing that everything will be alright. This is her story:

My friends always tease me during conversations of our childhood because I can hardly remember details of our lives that young. They'll have fresh memories of events that took place when we were 6, 10 or 13 and I won't have any idea of what they're talking about! I find it so strange because here I am in the latter years of my twenties and I still have very vivid memories of being 4 and 5 years old riding around with my Dad in our burgundy Chevy Lumina, him combing my hair into ponytails, and making the best homemade hamburgers I'd ever had until this day, it seems. My dad, he was to me what most Dads are to their little girls...EVERYTHING. One day I was sitting next to him, feeling proud and cherished, one arm around my protector, my hero, the only man I knew. The next day without warning, he was gone!

My Mom asked me to write my perception and personal emotions about how my Dad's absence affected my life. Growing up, I remember my parents fighting (arguing not physical fighting) some but not really fully understanding why. And when my Dad went to prison, it was devastating. As devastating as it was though, I recall only being concerned with how it affected my Mom. Even as young as I was, I could tell it was very difficult for her. My own emotions, I don't think I processed for some time later. Not until his absence started to really affect my life personally. I remember being made fun of and talked about in elementary school for not having a father around or for having a father that was in jail. Kids can be so cruel and it hurts, but my Mom made sure that we never wanted for anything and life was good as far as I was concerned. We always wore the nicest clothes and usually whatever my brother and I wanted, we got.

We went to visit my Dad frequently depending on where he was. We maintained a relationship with him even though he wasn't physically around. If we wanted to go somewhere or do something, my Mom would say "Wait until your Dad calls and ask him." I realized later that she did that because she wanted to keep my Dad included; allowing him to remain the head of his house. He called at least a couple of times a day usually but my Mom would use most of the time on the phone to keep him updated with our daily lives. There were times as I got older that I didn't like going on the visits because they would be used as disciplinary times for things we did the week or month prior to seeing my Dad. I used to think, "You weren't even there to know or understand!" How could he know or understand? I love my Dad so much but the older I got, the more I began to resent him for not being around. By the time he was released, that resentment and hurt had translated into un-forgiveness and disrespect. As much time as we spent with him, I still didn't feel like I knew him. When my Dad came home I was 18 years old and he had physically missed every single most important event in my life up to that point, and I was angry about it. It wasn't until my teenage years that my Dads absence really affected me. I lacked respect for my Mom because I felt like she should've moved on with her life; like she deserved better than my perception of the situation. I lacked respect for my Dad because I felt like he was selfish and if he had truly loved us, he wouldn't have made the decisions he made to end up in prison. I became rebellious and got a bit out of control. I think somewhere along the way I internalized a subconscious message that I wasn't good enough, I wasn't worthy of my Dads time and expected to be abandoned. Now that may sound farfetched to some, especially my parents because they've always shown me love and support. But now that I'm older I realize and understand things better about myself and some of the decisions that I've made in my life. Believe it or not; living helped me better understand my parents and the decisions they made. I truly understand it now without blame, judgment or un-forgiveness. I love them both dearly and I am so blessed and excited for the people they've become. My Dad and I have a great relationship and I've learned I'm more like him than I could've ever imagined. I'm so proud of the Man he is today.

After all is said and done, when the tears are gone and you peel back all of the layers of anger, confusion and frustration, you realize that you are your experiences. It makes you and I'm grateful for them, good and bad. My Dad dealt with his situations based upon his own level of awareness at the time. He did what he felt he needed to do and my Mom showed me what true unconditional love is outside of Christ. In the world we live in, it's hard to believe that it even exists. But it does and I'm a living witness.

I know many young girls and even adult women can relate to some of the things I've shared. Many of you may feel that some of the way I felt mirrors your own feelings. It's not an easy situation, but no hurt; no pain is too much for the healing power of God. I know it's true that, the Blood Jesus shed on Calvary STILL works! All you have to do is receive it. Un-forgiveness is a terrible thing to harbor in your heart. It's like a poison and if you don't get rid of it, it will cut you off from so many blessings to come into your life, cloud your vision of reality and even keep you from the Kingdom of Heaven. So if you're reading this and haven't already dealt with the un-forgiveness in your heart from earlier in the book, than I'm "begging" you! Please pray and ask God to heal you where you hurt. He healed me, so I know it's possible. Whoever you are, wherever you are and whatever your situation; God loves you and so do I. I extend my faith in agreement for you to receive your healing and God's absolute best for your life.

I hope that my daughter's story was helpful for you. I could've used a book like this when I was raising my children. There are some things that I certainly would have done differently, had I known what she was internalizing at the time, our other children as well. If your children are expressing some of these same behaviors or emotions, take time to talk with them and allow them to freely express how they feel. Explain to them what has happened and make sure they understand that they are not at fault in any way. It may help them to heal and possibly keep them from making a lot of unnecessary mistakes.

50 Shades of Brown: An Exchange of Love

A poetic expression of love dedicated to the love of my life Darren Brown.

Written by Poetic Praise Artists:
Ed & Shareda Rollins of **4HisWill**
facebook.com/edspokanvizion

50 Shades of Brown

Together

As I turn and look at you I cant help but see your many shades glow.
There is no sun but you light up every area of my life.
How did I come to love you so and how do you love me unconditionally?

Tonya

50 glances would not be enough to see the depth of who God said you are.
50 words could not express how I truly feel about the way you have changed my life forever.
50 dances would not be enough to share sweet nothings in your ear or wrap my arms around you tight.
50 days would seem like moments if that was all you had to give.

So give me 50 years.
50 years to build a kingdom with you,
50 nights to count the stars so we can see your
legacy displayed in God's design.
50 dreams to outline our road to success and
50 wishes each one I would wish that I could
spend the rest of my life holding you.
50 speeches and I would proclaim to the nations
how God made you just for me. 50 shades of
Brown.

Darren

You color me with your strength, your common
traits produce uncommon results making the
business of life extraordinary when you are
around my senses are aroused as I watch you
work and play I can smell the nectar of your labor
and its sweetest shade of brown.
Did you know that at the perfect moment caramel
light glistens in the corner of your eyes?
It is then that I see the visions you share with me.
I see the clarity of Gods perfect work in you.
I see the undying devotion you gave to me it is
then.

Tonya

I see the king you have always been.

Together

If I only had 50 thoughts I would daydream about
creating life with you.

If I had 50 skills I would use them to praise God for his work in molding you.

And, if I had 50 seconds left I would use each one kissing you!

Thank you for being my 50 shades of brown.

Make Contact!

After reading this book, take time out to write me or respond by following me on twitter:

@mrstonyabrown

And liking my Facebook page:

Facebook.com/AuthorTonyaBrown

I want to know what impact this book has had in your life! Tweet me if you're going to keep yourself for your husband and be sure to order your "I'M WORTH WAITING" FOR T-shirt! LET'S CHANGE THE WORLD LADIES ONE *"NO, I'M WORTH THE WAIT"* AT A TIME!

"I'VE REALIZED MY WORTH—JESUS FIRST!"

About Author Tonya Brown

Entrepreneur, Author, and Motivational Speaker Tonya Brown was born and raised in Kansas City, Missouri. Her life tells a story of hope and perseverance that is inspirationally geared towards encouraging women of all ages and backgrounds, but also young men.

At the age of fourteen, Tonya met her high school sweetheart Darren who would prove to play a major role in both her life and her purpose. Upon graduating high school the two had their first child together, were quickly wed, and balancing the life of responsibility and hardship. Tonya's world was turned upside down when her husband was hit with multiple prison sentences for his involvement with drug distribution leaving Tonya to rear their family alone. Forced to deal with a harsh new reality for her marriage and her family, Tonya drew strength from her devoutly rooted faith in God and His ability to sustain not only her husband, but her family and her new role as a "single" woman.

Tonya's unwavering love and prayers for her husband permeated prison bars and played an undeniable role in his radical sell out to Christ. Today the two enjoy the fullness of not only civil freedom but freedom in every area of their lives. They unanimously attribute their successes as entrepreneurs, authors, and community advocates to God's favor and love.

Tonya's sole mission is to help women understand that their value and self-worth is complete only in Christ, whether single, married, divorced, widowed, young or old. Her zeal for life and passion for helping others are remarkably evident in the sharing of personal testimony and service to others. Tonya's bold personality and candidness are as much a part of her charisma as her heart to make an impact on the Kingdom of God.

FROM RAGS, TO REDEMPTION
...TO REIGN!

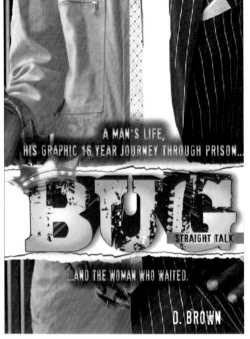

D. Brown's "Bug" is the highly acclaimed graphical autobiography about a convicted felon and the 16 years of incarceration that undeniably shaped not only his life, but his family's as well. Growing up in Kansas City, Missouri living an impoverished and often times unsupervised life, Bug became accustomed to making his own way early on. After high school, the Air Force and marrying his high school sweetheart, Bug soon found himself drawn to the hustle and affluence of the drug game. Risking his family and his life he became engrossed in the fast life of drugs, violence, and riotousness that abruptly ended in arrest, regret and 16 years to pay for. Filled with stories so graphic they have to be true, mind-blowing statistics about our country's social climate, and the taboo profitability of the penal system, you can't afford not to read, "Bug." Page by page, discover the story about a man whose beginnings were grim—but was destined for greatness. This book is an eye-opening story of how remorse can lead to redemption, how a wife's solitude can strengthen her devotion, and more importantly how those with similar stores can find hope.

DARREN BROWN
Author, Entrepreneur, & Community Activist

Darren Brown was born and raised in the heart of Kansas City, MO, in an impoverished and dangerous upbringing abandoned by his mother at 6 years old and rescued by his grandmother. Living an unsupervised life, caught in poverty's grip, Darren knew that life had more to offer than struggle, which led him to the streets of Kansas City at 11 years old, drawn to the hustle and affluence of the drug game as early as the sixth grade. After graduating from high school and marrying his high school sweetheart, risking his family and his life, he became engrossed in the fast life of drugs, violence, and riotousness that abruptly ended in arrest, regret, and 16 years of imprisonment to pay for.

Through Darren's life changing experience it is his heart, mandated by God, to save a posterity alive here on this earth! Darren's notoriety is most attributed to his new best-selling biography BUG "Straight Talk", a raw 16 year journey through some of the worst penitentiary's in America, and the woman who waited.

Darren is the president and founder of Wisdom Cries LLC, a non-profit organization that endeavors to impact the community through education, awareness, and pure wisdom. As a consultant in prison prevention and intervention, Darren's passion is reaching out to our children and young people through partnerships such as the Kansas City Missouri school district, the KCMO prosecutor's office, and many more. Darren Brown is open to speaking engagements, counseling, and interviews, including schools, men's conferences, and community organizations.

Follow D. Brown on Twitter:

@BugStraightTalk

Or Like him on Facebook:

Facebook.com/dbrown100

For more information about booking D. or Tonya Brown for speaking engagements, seminars, or about ordering "A Woman's Worth", "Bug: Straight Talk," or our Wisdom Cries LLC Organization, visit us online at
www.wisdomcries.info

Or write or call us!

Wisdom Cries LLC
22 E. 32nd St.
Kansas City, Missouri
64111-1106

(816) 561-2809